Dreaming of Home

Reimagining Ireland

Volume III

Edited by Dr Eamon Maher,
Technological University Dublin – Tallaght Campus

PETER LANG

Oxford • Bern • Berlin • Bruxelles • New York • Wien

Dreaming of Home

Seven Irish Writers

Gerald Dawe

PETER LANG

Oxford • Bern • Berlin • Bruxelles • New York • Wien

Bibliographic information published by Die Deutsche Nationalbibliothek. Die Deutsche Nationalbibliothek lists this publication in the Deutsche Nationalbibliografie; detailed bibliographic data is available on the Internet at http://dnb.d-nb.de.

A catalogue record for this book is available from the British Library.

Library of Congress Cataloging-in-Publication Data
Names: Dawe, Gerald, 1952- author.
Title: Dreaming of home : seven Irish writers / Gerald Dawe.
Description: Oxford ; New York : Peter Lang, 2022. | Series: Reimagining
    Ireland, 16629094 ; vol no.111 | Includes bibliographical references.
Identifiers: LCCN 2022006305 (print) | LCCN 2022006306 (ebook) |
    ISBN 9781800796553 (paperback) | ISBN 9781800796560 (ebook) |
    ISBN 9781800796577 (epub)
Subjects: LCSH: English literature—Irish authors—History and criticism. |
    Home in literature.
Classification: LCC PR8711 .D39 2022 (print) | LCC PR8711 (ebook) |
    DDC 820.9/9415—dc23/eng/20220310
LC record available at https://lccn.loc.gov/2022006305
LC ebook record available at https://lccn.loc.gov/2022006306

Cover image: Nevill Johnson Photographic Archives, RTE: '13a Stoneybatter, Dublin 1952/3'.
Cover design by Peter Lang Ltd.

ISSN 1662-9094
ISBN 978-1-80079-655-3 (print)
ISBN 978-1-80079-656-0 (ePDF)
ISBN 978-1-80079-657-7 (ePub)

© Peter Lang Group AG 2022

Published by Peter Lang Ltd, International Academic Publishers,
Oxford, United Kingdom
oxford@peterlang.com, www.peterlang.com

This publication has been peer reviewed.

For Brendan Kennelly, poet, teacher, friend

'To write poetry is to declare war on labels and clichés'

– Brendan Kennelly

Contents

Preface

Dreaming of Home is not a conventional academic study. There is no central thesis being set out, nor for that matter am I interested in proving an intellectual argument with a review of previous criticism, as is the case with most contemporary scholarly monographs. In keeping with the originals of these chapters, based on public lectures for a general audience which included hundreds of Irish Leaving Certificate students and their teachers, my intention is to convey as clearly and coherently as possible a 'way in' to the varied and, at times, complicated achievements of several Irish writers.

Ranging from the canonical status of Sean O'Casey and W. B. Yeats, the lectures – delivered over a span of fifteen and more years – were designed to encourage class participation, with discussion forming a lively and dynamic conclusion to the formal business of the lecture. So the reader should, to begin with, bear in mind the oral nature of these chapters, written as they were to be spoken. I have, however, tried to convert the sometimes repetitive shape of a lecture – rehearsing ground, privileging clarity, generalisation and conclusions – into the necessary priorities of interlinked chapters.

That said, I should point out that there is an underlying pattern in *Dreaming of Home*, though unforced and secondary to each of the individual studies. For the 'home' here is both an actual place, a physical house, a neighbourhood, a region as much as it is an imagined place, somewhere 'dreamed' about and either revered or contested and damaged as a result. What happens when these places – in this instance, a room in a Dublin tenement in the early decades of the twentieth century – is assailed by soldiers of an Irish revolutionary army? Fast forward fifty or sixty years and move to the north-west of the island, to Colette Bryce's Derry, and another 'conflict situation' involving civilians under attack this time by a (British) state army. Or move east and the violation of a family porch as a young family witness the brutal murder of their father in Gail McConnell's 1980s Belfast. These extremes of history bracket *Dreaming of Home* and within them life carries on as best it can. Yeats's fantasy of Miltonic splendour in Thoor Ballylee; Patrick Kavanagh's influential journey from the borderlands of Monaghan to Dublin in the early 1930s; John Montague's painful return from his boyhood family in New York to Garvaghey in County Tyrone, Derek Mahon's poems, these all muse on the very human desire for a place to call 'home'.

In the afterword, I place a favourite poem 'Asphodel, that greeny flower' by the American poet William Carlos Williams as a paradigm and comparison of how the personal and the political can be married into a poem of powerful resonance for today – the USA under internal fire from McCarthyite extremism and an uncertain grasp on world politics. The long poem, driven by formal control and a perfect management of line, metaphor and tone, closes the book on what is, I hope, a sense of replenishment and an offering of hope for the future in spite of what the worst can do. Poets and poetry dominate *Dreaming of Home* because this was the subject I was most often asked to speak about. Others much better qualified than I could well take this basic model and connect it to other forms of literary and indeed visual art. These essays were written in the hope of showing how the imagination can withstand the tyrannies of history by creating spaces where we can all meet and discover one another.

Acknowledgements

Earlier drafts of Chapters 1, 2, 4, 5 and 7 were delivered as public lectures in the Evening Lecture Series at Trinity College Dublin. Sections of Chapter 2 were included in a lecture given at 'Maud Gonne: The Muse of W. B. Yeats' Festival, Rossnaree, County Meath. Chapter 3 was given as an address at the Patrick Kavanagh Weekend in Inniskeen, County Monaghan and Chapters 6 and 7 were part of an extra-mural lecture series planned for 2020 but which did not take place due to the pandemic. All the material is unpublished and has been extensively rewritten for inclusion in *Dreaming of Home*.

The author would like to thank the organisers of the above lecture programmes, particularly Stephen Matterson, Lilian Foley, the late Ciaran Foley and Nicholas Grene (at TCD) and Brian Lynch (Patrick Kavanagh Weekend). A special thanks, too, to Conor Linnie for all his help with this and other publications.

Special acknowledgement to Peter Fallon, editor and publisher at The Gallery Press, for permission to include quotations from the work of John Montague and Derek Mahon, and to the literary estates of W. B. Yeats, Sean O'Casey and Patrick Kavanagh. The poetry of Colette Bryce is published by Picador and Gail McConnell's poetry by Green Bottle Press, Ink Sweat and Tears Press and Penned *in the Margins*, to all of whom kind thanks is due.

Dreaming of Home is dedicated to Brendan Kennelly, the source of inspiration, fun and great encouragement during my time at Trinity College Dublin from 1988 to 2017.

CHAPTER I

Precarious Refuges: Sean O'Casey

It is as plain as a pikestaff that Dublin is *not* at the core of Sean O'Casey's plays but a certain notion of Dublin based upon the lives of what we would now call the 'inner city'. The tenement reality, which fuses O'Casey's Abbey plays into such powerful operatic drama, is a ferociously selective part of the city. But it is little wonder that O'Casey could well have seen the tenement reality as the *only* reality. By 1900 when he was 20 years old, with six years of a working life behind him, 'fully one third of Dublin's population, some 21,747 families, lived in single-room dwellings in 6,196 tenements, many condemned by the Corporation as "unfit for human habitation"'.[1]

Dublin also had 'a higher proportion of poor than any other city in the British Isles as the rows of dilapidated tenement houses had become a 'traditional feature of the urban landscape'.[2] According to the same study, by 1900 the tenement houses 'then mostly between 100 and 150 years old, typically suffered from corroded brickwork, leaky roofs, sagging ceilings, rotting floor-boards and woodwork, cracked walls, crumbling fireplaces, broken windows, rickety staircases – general decay within and without'.[3]

What O'Casey achieved was to make it seem that this tenement life *was* Dublin when in fact the experiences, lifestyles and suffering of the tenement dwellers were, at the time of his writing the plays, still kept very much in the dark by official Ireland. Tenement reality, the very core of O'Casey's Abbey plays, was the anarchic, dangerous otherworld of city life.

---

1   Kevin C. Kearns, *Dublin Tenement Life: An Oral History* (Dublin: Gill & Macmillan, 2006), 8.

2   Kearns, *Dublin Tenement Life*, 8.

3   Kearns, 9.

O'Casey was not the first playwright to deal with tenement life. As
Nicholas Grene points out, 'There had been tenement plays before O'Casey,
notably *Blight* in 1917, by Oliver St. John Gogarty and Joseph O'Connor,
which was the first Abbey production O'Casey himself saw'.[4] But by mid-
twentieth century, Dublin would have been much more associated with
the image James Joyce presents of the city in *Dubliners*.[5] A class-bound,
snobbish, self-regarding society, knowledgeable, claustrophobic, provincial, stable and curiously alert to the hidden tensions that Joyce dramatises
with such precision in, for example, the exchange between Molly Ivors
and Gabriel Conroy in *The Dead* when she refers to the hapless Gabriel
as a 'West Briton'.[6]

In O'Casey's dramatic world, that lower middle-class lifestyle, which
he knew something of as a boy, is light years away. It is the world that
Mary Boyle in *Juno and the Paycock* yearns to inhabit; and that Nora in
The Plough and the Stars impersonates. It is the world that the 'Lady from
Rathmines' in *The Plough* strays from and the world that the Boyle family
can only parody in their brief illusory moment in the sun. 'We'll han' the
tea round', says Juno, 'an' not be clusthered round the table, as if we never
seen nothin''.[7] Joxer and the Captain belong literally to a different world
where a single sausage is breakfast, 'it may be the last you'll get', Juno remarks, 'for I don't know where the next is goin' to come from'.[8]

In the Captain's world the pub opens early and the drinking rarely
stops; where women with absent husbands, who always look older than
their years, work as best they can at whatever they can; and if there is no
work, they pawn whatever little bits and pieces of furniture or personal
effects they possess, to get by. When that no longer works, they hit either
the bottle or a neighbour in consuming rage.

4   Nicholas Grene, *The Politics of Irish Drama: Plays in Context from Boucicault to
     Friel* (Cambridge: Cambridge University Press, 1999), 111.
5   James Joyce, *Dubliners* (London: Jonathan Cape 1934 [original pub. 1914]).
6   James Joyce, 'The Dead', *Dubliners* (London: Jonathan Cape, 1934), 216.
7   All quotations from Sean O'Casey, *Three Dublin Plays*, introduced by Christopher
     Murray (London: Faber and Faber, 1998), 103.
8   O'Casey, *Three Dublin Plays,* 77.

The 'slum lice',[9] as Captain Brennan, chicken butcher and captain of the Irish Citizen Army, refers to the tenement dwellers in *The Plough* are a community unto themselves. Those who try to break rank, like Nora, are punished for so trying – initially by the mocking tone of their own neighbours but ultimately, alas, by losing their bearings on where they are. The powerful apocalyptic moments in O'Casey's Abbey plays are precisely when the fabric of the wider city is ruptured and the reality behind comes bursting through as plunder and looting take hold in bizarre, unpredictable flashes[10]:

> *Bessie runs in excitedly She has a new hat on her head, a fox fur round her neck over her shawl, three umbrellas under her right arm and a box of biscuits under her left.*
>
> *She speaks rapidly and breathlessly.*
>
> Bessie   They're breakin'into th'shops, they're breakin' into th' shops! Smashin' th'windows, batterin' in th' doors, an' whippin' away everything! An' the Volunteers is firin' on them. I seen two men an' a lassie pushin' a piano down th' sthreet, an' th' sweat rollin' off them thryin' to get it up on th'pavement' an' an oul' wan that must ha' been seventy lookin' as if she'd dhrop every minute with th' dint o' heart beatin', thryin' to pull a big double bed out of a broken shop window! I was goin' to wait till I dhressed meself from the skin out.
>
> *Mollser (to Bessie, as she is going in)* Help me in, Bessie' I'm feelin' curious.

A marvellously funny scene but also, as is the case so often with O Casey, the tragic reality is never too far below the surface. But what was that tenement world really like? In Jacinta Prunty's essay 'From City Slums to City Sprawl: Dublin from 1800 to the Present', the best summary I have of the tenement system, the following extract reveals with stunning effect the shocking conditions the people had to endure[11]:

> Usually four storeys in height, there was no direct means of removing the refuse from each floor, so that the common stairs soon became fouled, and the provision of piped water and bathrooms to each unit was impractical. A toilet in an outside

9   O'Casey, 219.
10   O'Casey, 211–212.
11   Jacinta Prunty, 'From City Slums to City Sprawl: Dublin from 1890 to the Present', *Irish Cities,* edited by Howard Clarke (Cork: Mercier Press, 1995), 115–118 [116].

yard shared by fifteen or sixteen families was difficult to keep clean, particularly when anyone could come in off the street and use it.

Prunty's portrait of dreadful unhygienic housing conditions reveals an even more shocking truth – and subject of much speculation too – in the economic ladders of commercial interest which lay at the foundations of such an inhumane system. 'In the complex web of Dublin property holding, with perhaps five owners to one tenement house along with immediate lessees, tenants, subtenants and occupiers, it was often impossible to determine who was responsible for repairs.' This confluence of little return and studied neglect produced further and irrevocable damage: 'Enforcing health regulations often led to more distress, as the former tenants, unable to pay higher rents for the improved dwellings, overcrowded other tenements.' In such circumstances, as Prunty's work powerfully reveals, the social structure of Dublin (and Irish) life was economically perverse: 'In a city in which there was so little remunerative employment "house jobbing", or the subletting of property, was an important source of income among the poor as well as among the better-off.' For the generation of O'Casey's characters, the reality was overwhelming: 'these circumstances', Prunty comments, 'were not all confined to a small if distressed section of the population; over one-third of the citizens lived in such unacceptable conditions in 1894.'[12]

Such conditions would naturally have direct health implications and in Kevin C. Kearns's study, *Dublin Tenement Life: An Oral History* the situation is spelt out in graphic detail[13]:

> The living conditions of many tenement dwellers were hellish. Their buildings were decayed, dangerous, and sometimes collapsed, killing occupants. Some tenement areas had 800 people to the acre, as many as a hundred persons in one house, and fifteen to twenty family members in a single tiny room. A primitive toilet and water tap in the rear yard had to serve all the inhabitants of a house. Amid such suffocating humanity and lack of sanitation it is small wonder that the tenements were condemned [.]

12   Prunty, 'From City Slums to City Sprawl', 116.
13   Kearns, 2.

And in case we get carried away with the time-honoured notion that British culpability is written all over these social conditions, Kearns reminds us that 'Dublin slums existed well into the late 1940s, a powerful indictment of government neglect and ineptitude'.[14] As he makes clear throughout his history of 'slum' life, the most prevalent illnesses were 'tuberculosis, diphtheria, smallpox, typhoid, pneumonia, whooping cough, respiratory ailments, rheumatic arthritis, and diarrhoeal diseases. Contagious diseases naturally spread like wildfire amid such congestion. Tuberculosis sometimes wiped out entire families. Sickness and premature death were an accepted part of life in the tenements.'[15]

Alongside these dreadful conditions, a self-autonomous world of super-stitions and wakes, gambling and what were known as 'animal' gangs, of courting and marriage, childbirth and premature pregnancy ('regarded' Kearns remarks, 'as high scandal and a moral plight upon the girl's family'),[16] entertainment and street life. Religion was the social cement; all the various reports dealing with tenement life found it the most lasting influence, even as late as the 1930s. The Church, it seems, had no equal as it was considered 'the central core of their daily life'[17]:

> In a world of physical hardship, financial struggles, illness, and alcoholism, tenement women bore the greatest burdens. When times were roughest they instinctively turned to their religion for comfort.

The sharpest (and tragic) irony here is that, alongside this powerful presence of the Church in Dublin, prostitution was also quite public and open in the inner city, as (again) Kearns makes clear 'some tenement areas were well-known as red-light districts, famed for their brothels ... Many prostitutes who lived in the tenements also plied their trade on O'Connell Street and Grafton Street where well-to-do gentlemen abounded. In fact a custom grew in O'Connell Street whereby one side of the street was re-served for "respectable" people and the other side for prostitutes.'[18] No

14   Kearns, 2.
15   Kearns, 13.
16   Kearns, 45.
17   Kearns, 43.
18   Kearns, 54.

wonder, then, that Joseph O'Brien in his study, *'Dear Dirty Dublin': A City in Distress, 1899–1916* remarks, 'through the very high rate of mortality (the highest of all the large towns and cities) Dublin maintained the unenviable reputation of being the unhealthiest city in the United Kingdom.'[19] Now my point is that all this social background is at the critical centre of Sean O'Casey's work but not as a *passive* backdrop, as scene-setting or as context; this social world *is* the actual structure of O'Casey's dramatisations. His plays and the inner city are one.

So let me give a fairly direct physical example of what I mean, noticed previously by D. E. S. Maxwell and also noted, incidentally, by none other than Samuel Beckett in a review[20] of O'Casey's *Windfalls* (1934). This is Maxwell describing O'Casey's stage world[21]:

> It is a world of pratfalls that collect into an image of a disintegrating society, a world whose nature is to fall apart. Its habitation, oddly, is the insistent, seedy solidity of O'Casey's prescriptions for his stage: walls, chairs, tables, fireplaces, precisely detailed, whose point is that they are unreliable and vulnerable. The directions are novelistic to the extent of describing items which are no longer, but have been, there – in *The Plough* the fireplace 'of wood, painted to look like marble (the original has been taken away by the landlord'); so detailed, so visible to O'Casey's imagination, that, like the pub scene in the same play, they leave little to the stage designer's initiative. All, in the end, are merely precarious refuges. Here it is that the political voice must make itself heard.

The very fabric of O'Casey's plays speaks of Dublin and its history through those 'precarious refuges'. As William Irwin Thompson describes it, the action of Act Three of *The Plough and the Stars* takes place in a public street just outside 'a great house, but here, significantly, the great house, an old Georgian mansion, is a tenement with not a single pane of glass remaining in the once elegant tracery of the fanlight. Against this

---

19   Joseph V. O'Brien, *'Dear Dirty Dublin': A City in Distress, 1899–1916* (California: University of California Press, 1992), 105.

20   Samuel Beckett, 'The Essential and the Incidental', *Disjecta: Miscellaneous Writings and a Dramatic Fragment*, edited with a foreword by Ruby Cohn (London: John Calder, 1983), 82–83.

21   D. E. S. Maxwell, *Modern Irish Drama* (Cambridge: Cambridge University Press, 1984), 100.

background of the past (and, one infers, of a past social order) gone to ruin, the slum dwellers come and go as the insurrection blazes and thunders off stage.'[22]

Is this why W. B. Yeats was so much in love with the Big House because so many in Dublin had fallen to rack and ruin in his mind's eye? If the physical structure of O'Casey's plays dramatise the tenement life how much more so do the characters embody with a shocking unselfconsciousness the lives of harsh struggle? It may be useful to remind ourselves who some of those main characters are, including the playwright himself.

O'Casey was 43 when the Abbey accepted *The Shadow of a Gunman* and the play was given a run of four nights in April 1923. As Christopher Morash reminds us,[23] the play opened two days after Liam Lynch, the leader of the anti-Treaty IRA, was shot dead by Free State forces. The following year (March 1924) *Juno and the Paycock* was performed and became the most popular play in the Abbey's twenty-year history and a boost to its perilous finances. Two years later, in February 1926, riots greeted O'Casey's *The Plough and the Stars* on its fourth night and in March of the same year he moved to England where he was to remain for the rest of his long life.

Again Morash makes the telling point that 'during that tempestuous winter of 1926' both 'O Casey's play [*The Plough*] and [Eamon] de Valera's decision to enter the Dáil were part of the same process of learning to live with the revolutionary energies of preceding decades'.[24]

In 1928 The Abbey rejected *The Silver Tassie*, though the company made amends in 1935 with a production (which also caused a bit of a stir) and again in 1951. And of the characters O'Casey created, the facts speak for themselves, as Lady Gregory had stated when she first read his work.

In *The Plough and the Stars* the main characters are surprisingly young: Jack, a bricklayer, is 25, his pregnant wife, Nora, is 22 – 'alert, swift, full of nervous energy' –her uncle, Peter Flynn, 'a little thin bit of a man' is a labourer and 40ish. Clitheroe's cousin, The Covey, is 25 and a fitter.

22 William Irwin Thompson, *The Imagination of an Insurrection: Dublin Easter 1916* (New York: Oxford University Press, 1967), 218.

23 Christopher Morash, *A History of Irish Theatre, 1601–2000* (Cambridge: Cambridge University Press, 2002), 174.

24 Morash, *A History of Irish Theatre*, 171.

Bessie Burgess, a fruit vendor, is 40 (vigorously built somewhat like Mrs Henderson in *The Shadow of a Gunman*, 'a massive woman'). Mrs Gogan, also 40, a charwoman, is described as 'a doleful-looking little woman' with a consumptive daughter, Mollser, 15 who dies of the disease. Fluther Good, a carpenter, is 40, while Rose Redmond, a prostitute, is only 20.

In comparison with the main characters in *Juno and the Paycock*, the characters in *The Plough* seem at least to be working, even from the very first scene as Fluther is repairing the lock of Nora Clitheroe's door, much to Bessie's disfavour ('Afraid her poor neighbours ud breakthrough an' steal … Maybe now they're a damn sight more honest than your lady-ship'[25]). Indeed Nora's notions of 'upperousity'[26] vex both Bessie and, in that opening scene, Mrs Gogan, with the implication that she, Nora, is looking down upon the others – 'She thries to be polite'[27] – and even the sexual energy that Nora displays is frowned upon by Mrs Gogan – 'To see her, sometimes of an evenin' in her glad-neck gown would make a body's blood run cold'.[28] But by play's end this group of striving, troubled, hugely animated people are consumed in tragedy.

And here we can see forcefully where all those cold statistics take on flesh and blood of dramatised reality. Mrs Gogan's daughter is dead, like her husband, of consumption. (Incidentally, this is the disease that Captain Boyle momentarily believes his daughter Mary to have contracted.) Nora has lost her reason and miscarried her baby which will be buried within the same coffin as Mollser. Nora's husband is shot dead, as is Lieutenant Langon and Bessie, shot protecting the 'uppety' Nora – 'You bitch, you' cries Bessie in her death struggle. The men who remain are interned, parts of the city are in flames and the final scene of British soldiers drinking tea and singing 'Keep the home fires burning' is really an apocalyptic vision of an Irish society that had just passed through the crisis of Easter 1916 into history.

In comparison the characters in *Juno*, based on the later events of the civil war of 1922, are more accepting of their fate, less eager to forge

25   O'Casey, 167.
26   O'Casey, 153.
27   O'Casey, 154.
28   O'Casey, 154.

a new life, although Mary and Jerry Devine come close to Nora in this
regard. Mary Boyle, ('ever since she left school', Juno remarks proudly
of her daughter, 'she's earned her living'[29]) is on strike. Like Nora in *The
Plough*, she tries to read her way into a better life. She demonstrates a desire
to change things but 'Captain' Boyle, the father who hasn't worked a full
week in his entire life, will have none of it[30]:

> Boyle　Her an' her readin'! That's more o' th' blasted nonsense that has the house
> fallin' down on top of us! What did th' likes of her, born in a tenement house,
> want with readin'? Her readin's afther bringin' her to a nice pass – oh, it's madnin',
> madnin', madnin'!

Boyle is 'about sixty', Juno 45, Mary 25 and her destroyed brother Johnny
'something younger'. Joxer Daly may be younger than his Captain 'but
looks older'. Masie Madigan is 45, Mrs Tancred 'a very old woman' and
both suitors for Mary are 25 – Jerry Devine, the trade unionist, and
the schoolteacher, Charles Bentham. Boyle, Joxer and Johnny are un-
employed or unemployable. But it is the description of Juno which is the
most damning in the play: 'She must have been a pretty women but her
face has now assumed that look of listless monotony and harassed anxiety, blending with an expression of mechanical resistance. Were circumstances favourable, she would probably be a handsome, active and clever
woman.'[31] But the circumstances are not 'favourable'.

　　In fact they are going to get much worse as the play unfolds from that
early stage description. Her son will be executed for the crime of betraying
his former comrades, although why he acted the way he did remains a little
unclear. Her daughter becomes pregnant and ultimately flees under Juno's
protection. Her husband descends deeper into self-delusion on a drunken
wave of his old butty's mishmash of songs and stories. 'The last o' the
Mohicans'[32] just about sums them up. Violence and death – of other sons
and husbands – will rock the tenement and district she lives in[33]:

29　O'Casey, 134.
30　O'Casey, 134–135.
31　O'Casey, 68.
32　O'Casey, 147.
33　O'Casey, 116–117.

Juno Hasn't the whole house, nearly, been massacreed? There's young Dougherty's husband with his leg off; Mrs Travers that had her son blew up be a mine in Incheegela in Co Cork; Mrs Mannin that lost wan of her sons in an ambush a few weeks ago, and now, poor Mrs Tancred's only child gone west with his body made a collandher of.

And all this will come after cruel fate has dangled momentarily before Juno's family a fleeting chance of a better way of life. Even after the possibility of the Will is snatched away from her by the blundering ways of her daughter's seducer, Juno sees this fate full-on, with no illusions: 'Now I know why Bentham left poor Mary in th' lurch. I can see it all now – Oh, is there not even a middli' honest man left in th' world?'[34]

If you look around at the men in these two plays, the answer to Juno's question is an emphatic No – not if you come from the tenements. Only the women – complicated and angry and hard done by as they mostly are – offer to one another some degree of consolation: 'My poor little child', laments Mary, 'that'll have no father!' To which Juno responds emphatically: 'It'll have what's far betther, it'll have two mothers.'[35]

So the city becomes a part of the city and the part of the city becomes a once grand house converted into rooms for parts of families, communes, if you like, run by women, defiant and vulnerable in turn, while their men are elsewhere. And the rooms are themselves partitioned into bits of rooms, like some kind of surreal habitation of the mind. It is a powerfully imagined dramatisation and indictment – but where does it leave us in present-day Dublin?

In the century which separates the original productions of Sean O'Casey's Abbey plays from us today there has been immense economic and social change in Ireland. On issues such as housing, for example, comparatively few live in the conditions of the tenement dwellers. The appalling inertia of Irish society has been transformed. The Catholic Church does not exert anything like the influence it did in O'Casey's time. The state is completely grounded in every facet of Irish life – if not completely acceptable to all. The hegemony of O'Casey's 'Dublin' no longer exists, however, and the political contours of cultural nationalism are much hazier now that

34   O'Casey, 136.
35   O'Casey, 146.

they ever were. The multi-cultural tensions of a different kind of Dublin are in evidence in a style and manner inconceivable in the 1920s.

The moral questions that O'Casey poses about ordinary life, the agencies of change and the politics of violence remain very potent in Irish life in general, most noticeably in the decades since his death in 1964. One thinks of placing some of his characters in present-day settings. The fate of Mary Boyle in a 'single parent' family; Johnny Boyle as one of 'the disappeared', dumped and buried along the border; the drug-ravaged inner city communities scarred by systemic unemployment going back as far as Boyle and before him. While the Pearsesian dream of 'The Figure in the Window' in *The Plough and the Stars* was such a lethal factor in the deaths of over 3,000 people in the Northern 'Troubles'. The corruption and insider dealing of Charles Bentham an anticipation of what would become exposed post Celtic Tiger collapse .... History is *never* over.

Sean O'Casey's achievement in his Abbey plays should be read at least comparatively with what has been achieved in dramatic terms after him; of how Irish playwrights developed and engaged with the kind of realities his plays comprehensively embodied, not as interesting 'issues', 'angles' or 'themes' but as ways of life passionately imagined for the stage as plays.

As a mediating theatrical presence, it is fair to say that no one individual has been in a position to interpret Dublin (or indeed Irish reality) with the kind of cultural authority that Sean O'Casey once possessed in his great Abbey plays. This change has clearly a lot to do with various social factors aligned to other changes in Irish society itself – the shrinking of theatre audiences, the diminishing of theatre as a privileged platform for and of debate, the mantra of product marketing, the impact upon much cultural activity of 'event management', the colossal shift in fashion towards cinema and video come to mind.

The cultural presence of the Abbey Theatre itself as 'the' national theatre is probably more fictional in twenty-first century Dublin than actual, a hangover from an earlier more coherent time which simply no longer exists. In a way, the whole concept of a 'national' theatre – or national literature, for that matter – may well need to be reimagined with a critical start made from scratch with the priorities and possibilities of the present city and country firmly in mind as they are today.

CHAPTER 2

In the Mind's Eye: W. B. Yeats

I

I plan to think aloud in what follows about W. B. Yeats's poetry, as a poet and reader myself and to look at some of his best-known and much-taught poems as illustrations of what a younger reader can expect to find in Yeats; pointing out what Yeats does with language, some ideas that mattered to him, the themes from his earliest days that he kept coming back to. For instance, as a young man in his 20s, living in London and writing 'The Lake Isle of Innisfree', a song of emigration if ever there was one, through to the rich vein of politically charged poems he wrote in his 40s and early 50s (poems such as 'September 1913', 'Easter 1916' and 'Meditations in Time of Civil War') along with the slightly weird reaches of 'The Second Coming' and 'Sailing to Byzantium', taking a brief look at the poems he wrote in late middle age and old age ('In Memory of Eva Gore-Booth and Con Markiewicz', 'An Acre of Grass' and 'Politics') before concluding with Yeats's influence on some poets who came after him.

I have divided these poems into four rough categories or themes: land-scape and longing, in which I have placed 'The Lake Isle of Innisfree', 'The Wild Swans at Coole' and 'An Acre of Grass'; politics: 'September 1913', 'Easter 1916', 'The Stare's Nest by my Window' and 'Politics'; the tran-scendent and visionary: 'The Second Coming', 'Sailing to Byzantium' and 'Swift's Epitaph' and finally commemoration: 'An Irish Airman Foresees his Death', 'In Memory of Eva Gore-Booth and Con Markiewicz' and the two concluding sections from 'Under Ben Bulben'.

Landscape and longing takes us from the 23-year-old in London in 1888, to the 53-year-old in Coole Park in Galway in 1918 and ends with the 71-year-old in Riversdale, Rathfarnham, Yeats's last residence in Ireland,

in 1936 towards the end of his life. The first thing I want to say here is the
most obvious. Each one of these poems is based in one place and either
looks back to some other place or time, other than the here and now of
the poem. Yeats from his earliest writing in 'The Lake Isle' to (almost) the
end of his writing life in 'An Acre of Grass' is haunted by the past, by what
might have been. At the heart of his poetry, there is generally a portrait
of himself, or version of himself, at a critical point of decision-making, of
weighing up things, of resolution – concerning lost loves, a way of life that
is vanishing (like Gaelic Ireland, the Anglo-Irish world, or the unspoilt
countryside) – or angry that he is himself vanishing – getting old –and
witnessing the weakening of his poetic energies.

Look at the connectedness of these lines, separated by almost fifty years:

> I will arise and go now, for always night and day
> I hear lake water lapping, with low sounds by the shore;
> While I stand on the roadway, or on the pavements grey,
> I hear it in the deep heart's core[1].

So the London boy 'will arise' (but has not!) while in 'An Acre of Grass',
the old man in 'an old house/Where nothing stirs but a mouse' is raging
against the fact that time has passed and 'the truth' of life, whatever that is, is
not 'known', yet he longs nonetheless to 'pierce the clouds' as the great artist
Michelangelo had; the mood of dreamy longing might have changed from
bees and linnet wings and cricket sounds to shrouds and eagles and frenzy
but the discontented troubled mind is there from the very beginning.

As a poet, Yeats is always testing the ground of the here and now;
always asking questions of himself, even at the very end of his life. That
is an astonishing recognition, I think; there is nothing complacent about
this poet because he never 'gives up'. When he said of 'The Lake Isle of
Innisfree' – that it was his 'first lyric with anything of my own music in it'
and that the poem uses 'nothing but common syntax',[2] Yeats was of course

1   All quotations are taken from *W. B. Yeats The Poems*, edited by Daniel Albright
     (London: J. M. Dent & Sons, 1990), 'The Lake Isle of Innisfree', 60.
2   W. B. Yeats, 'Four Years: 1887–1891', *Autobiographies* (London: Macmillan, 1980
     [1955]), 153.

right. Because it is clear he wrote in an English we can all understand; there is little in it which is not *speech-based*. Look at 'The Wild Swans at Coole', set in a specific place, and listen to how Yeats almost quotes himself from the earlier 'Innisfree' poem.

> I have looked upon those brilliant creatures
> And now my heart is sore.
> All's changed since I, hearing at twilight,
> The first time on this shore,
> The bell-beat of their wings above my head,
> Trod with a lighter tread.[3]

As you can see, 'shore' and 'heart's core' are in Innisfree; 'heart is sore' and 'this shore' in Coole, and, while we're at it, 'All's changed' turns up again in 'Easter 1916'. But the important point to note here is again the most obvious, the most direct: just how simple and colloquial the language is; this is how we speak English in Ireland (or maybe how we once spoke it.)

For Yeats (and this is critical to note) there are certain 'buzz-words' which set him off, or which he cannot quite leave out of his poems. Words that carry an emotional (personal) freight, and as 'The Wild Swans at Coole' gathers momentum, like the swans themselves, the words leave behind the everyday world of the personal and private recollections, and by their very *beautifulness*, take flight and take the reader to a wider vision or landscape. So the resonance of individual words sounds through his poems like a mantra. The word 'cloud' and 'clouds', for instance, shows up a lot in Yeats. They are there in 'An Acre of Grass' and they recur in 'Easter 1916' ('cloud to tumbling cloud') and in 'An Irish Air Man foresees his Death' ('the clouds above' and 'the tumult in the clouds'). So here is something basic too about the images Yeats make out of these individual words. They gather significance the more we catch on to them; they become 'iconic', to use a somewhat hackneyed word of today.

If we move on and have a brief look at the second pool of poems, under the theme of politics, we can see just how much of Yeats's middle years were taken up with Irish society – the immediate world around him,

3   Yeats, 'The Wild Swans at Coole', 180.

that is. Precious wonder too that those poems such as 'September 1913', 'Easter 1916' and 'Meditations in Time of Civil War' and 'Politics' should actually sound like a man talking, addressing someone directly who (or prospectively) is listening; an audience that the poet has in mind and who, he believes, needs to hear a thing or two.

This is the argumentative Yeats, who was happy for a fight, in fact was sometimes spoiling for one. Here Yeats is button-holing the reader, pointing an accusatory finger at you and me and at our failure to revere and respect the patriotic idealism of certain Irishmen who, at different times in our history, stood up against materialistic values of self-interest and personal gain. To read 'September 1913' is to recognise the voice that Yeats is impersonating in the poem, the voice of common moral outrage, disillusionment, even bitterness, and turned again a certain class of Irish people, spoken from the frontline: 'What need you, being come to sense, / But fumble in a greasy till / And add the halfpence to the pence/ And prayer to shivering prayer, until/ You have dried the marrow from the bone ... .'[4]

In the slightly later 'Easter 1916', which starts off (again in a definite place) in Dublin and moves out to an imagined countryside of horses and hounds, before returning to the fate of individually named men executed in the capital for their leading role in the 1916 Rising, it is important to *hear* the form of direct address, for again it is the sound of a man talking, at least in the opening of the poem: 'I have met them at close of day/ Coming with vivid faces/ From counter or desk among grey/ Eighteenth-century houses.'[5]

'Easter 1916' is more complicated than 'September 1913' but the poems are linked by this emphasis which Yeats had taken to heart from early on in his writing of poems, that it was his voice that mattered. He stopped imitating others and fashioned his own distinctive voice. The poem was a dramatic way of saying things and when he shifts focus away from the spoken voice in 'Easter 1916', we seem to enter into the poet's head, literally, and start to overhear his thoughts, as the poem becomes a soliloquy; an inner voice: 'Hearts with one purpose alone/ Through summer and winter seem/ Enchanted to a stone/ To trouble the living stream.'[6]

4   Yeats, 'September, 1913', 159.
5   Yeats, 'Easter, 1916', 228.
6   Yeats, 'Easter, 1916', 229.

This makes 'Easter 1916' much more of a hallucinogenic poem, as if we were in the middle of an interior monologue. And we are also back to another one of those Yeatsian buzz words – 'hearts'. But there is also the cloud and shadow of cloud. And there are 'the stones' of 'The Wild Swans at Coole' imagined here as well: 'Enchanted to a stone' and 'The stone's in the midst of all'. 'Easter 1916', like 'September 1913', responds in different ways to Yeats's own reactions to developments in Irish life during the decade of the 1910s. By the end of the decade he was depressed, unwell, his nerves wrecked. He had failed in marriage plans, twice, and all the 'talk', and idealism of his earlier manhood, seemed to have led him into a cul-de-sac.

The poems he collected into the volume *Responsibilities* (1914) and *The Wild Swans at Coole* (1919) include several poems about the cultural politics of the time. But he was also saddened about the loss of family friends, such as Lady Gregory's nephew, Hugh Lane, who had died when the Germans torpedoed the *Lusitania* in 1915 and her only son, Major Robert Gregory who was killed in action in First World War in 1918. And there was his shock at the execution between these private griefs of the leaders of the Rising in 1916, many of whom were personally known to him. 'September 1913' and 'Easter 1916' are poems that mark both the anger and shock at what is going on around him. He even uses some of the language of the time; for instance, in 'Easter 1916' in the headlining wishfulness of 'England May Keep Faith' – which was not to be.

In the post-First World War Ireland, Yeats could not help but see how the voices of his generation of idealistic nationalists were being increasingly drowned out by the military campaigns of militant Irish republicans – first in the War of Independence and tragically in the internecine Civil War, the backdrop to Yeats's greatest sequence of poems, 'Meditations in Time of Civil War'. This is how Yeats described the background to his sequence:

> I was in my Galway house during the first months of civil war, the railway bridges blown up and the roads blocked with stones and trees. For the first week there were no newspapers, no reliable news, we did not know who had won nor who had lost, and even after newspapers came, one never knew what was happening on the other side of the hill or of the line of trees. For cars passed the house from time to time with coffins standing upon one end between the seats, and sometimes at night we

heard an explosion, and once by day saw the smoke made by the burning of a great neighbouring house. [7]

In the sixth section of the sequence, 'The Stare's Nest by my Window' curious echoes or reverberations appear. Here the Innisfree 'hive for the honey-bee' and the associated peacefulness of longing is brought up against a time of destruction and war.

> A barricade of stone or of wood;
> Some fourteen days of civil war;
> Last night they trundled down the road
> That dead young soldier in his blood … .[8]

The conflict between creation and destruction, life and death, solitude and the demands of communal strife are prefigured in much of 'Meditations … ' where, it should also be noted, the central image is of a house – Yeats's Thoor Ballylee in County Galway. The bees 'build' what in Innisfree had been the poet's 'cabin' and the nest of the starling is 'the empty house' of what would be in 'An Acre of Grass' 'an old house'. The domestic familial world embodied in the house is threatened by war's alarms.

Houses mattered to Yeats; he lived and stayed in very many of them – in Dublin, Sligo, Galway, London, the south of France; he restored that tower in Galway (from where he surveyed the civil war at first hand). And of course he wrote poems about houses, comparing them to living things; such as Lissadell, the focal point in his moving commemorative poem, 'In Memory of Eva Gore-Booth and Con Markiewicz'.

It might be appropriate at this point, though, to recall that Yeats himself, looking back at the very end of his life, in the poem 'Politics', wistfully and, perhaps mischievously, warned his reader against losing sight of the individual experience of life, and, looking back on his own life, maybe felt that he had spent too much time and energy on politics and the culture wars. In a letter he wrote that 'Politics', the poem, is 'not a real incident but

---

7   Yeats, 'The Bounty of Sweden', *Autobiographies*, 581.
8   Yeats, 'The Stare's Nest by my Window', 251.

a moment of meditation.'[9] Here is the telling conclusion to the poem: '…
maybe what they say is true / Of war and war's alarms,/ But O that I were
young again / And held her in my arms.'[10]

Yeats's poetry swings from one position to another, like a metronome.
While cautioning against wasteful politics, in 'Politics', Yeats had other
ideas about social order and the role of the imagination in the making of
history in poems such as 'The Second Coming' and 'Sailing to Byzantium'.
These constitute our third theme – as visionary and transcendent readings,
particularly of the place Yeats imagined his poems would inhabit, as well
as propounding very questionable notions of human civilisation.

'The Second Coming' is included in *Michael Robartes and the Dancer*
(1921). It is a collection of intensely political reflections on the upheavals
of Irish public life – poems such as 'Easter 1916', 'Sixteen Men Dead', 'The
Rose Tree', 'On a Political Prisoner', 'The Leaders of the Crowd' and 'A
Meditation in Time of War'. There is also a series of self-dramatisations
about 'childish memories of an old cross Pollexfen,/And of a Middleton,
whose name you never heard,/And of a red-haired Yeats whose looks, although he died/Before my time, seem like a vivid memory.'[11]

With the birth of his daughter Anne in 1919, Yeats was, perhaps,
brought back to his own childhood and the connections with Sligo, the
west of Ireland and to the tower he was to restore 'with old mill boards
and sea-green slates'.[12] The apocalyptic vision of 'The Second Coming' as
the nightmarish is placed alongside the image of birth and domesticity,
is focussed upon 'a rocking cradle' which brings forth an awesome image
of almost perverse transformation: 'what rough beast … /Slouches towards Bethlehem to be born?' Thinking of births and deaths seems to
have taken Yeats into some bizarre territory indeed, 'somewhere in sands
of the desert/ A shape with lion body and the head of a man,/… while
all about it/ Reel shadows of the indignant desert birds.'[13] Similarly, in

9   W. B. Yeats, *Letters on Poetry from W. B. Yeats to Dorothy Wellesley* (London: Oxford
      University Press, 1964), 163.
10   Yeats, 'Politics', 395.
11   Yeats, 'Under Saturn', 227.
12   Yeats, 'To Be Carved on a Stone at Thoor Ballylee', 238.
13   Yeats, 'The Second Coming', 235.

'Sailing to Byzantium', Yeats is thinking about what he himself called 'the state of his soul'. I suppose it is not uncommon for the mind of men and women in their early 60s to start thinking of their own mortality, and of what life actually amounts to. Certainly from the opening line of 'Sailing to Byzantium', Yeats dramatises an imaginary journey from one place of youth and creativity to another 'soul-landscape'.[14] But as I have previously mentioned, it is useful to see the journey in 'Sailing to Byzantium' from an Ireland of salmon going upstream to spawn, as in Galway's Salmon Weir, to the holy centre of European civilisation, in Byzantium, as the longing trip of the imagination.

Where is it we as individuals most want to see? What place is the place of our imaginations? For the cultured Yeats it happened to be a dream of artifice, like something John Keats would have imagined. And in both these poems Yeats engaged with the upside and downside of our wishes. So let me move on to the fourth and final theme of commemoration, one of the strongest motifs in Yeats's poetry. It was something he was doing from a very early age, if we think of 'The Lake Isle' as a poem commemorating his longing for another place, back home in Ireland. While there are numerous poems in which Yeats commemorates friends who have died, as well as times and places which 'have passed' or ceased to exist except in his recollection of them in his mind's eye.

For Yeats is the great poet of companionship and commemoration. We can see how he translates 'loss' – through death, ageing, disagreement – into a lasting thing in the art of memory: poetry not as testimony, but as its own physical, verbal monument to the human values which he (like a sculptor working with stone) wants to remind us of, as permanent, history-transcending virtues. Loss brought out the protestant in him.

'An Irish Air Man Foresees his Death' was included in the same volume as 'The Wild Swans at Coole'. It is one of four poems Yeats wrote about his friend Lady Gregory's only child, Robert Gregory, a major in the Royal Air Corps. He had died at the Italian Front during First World War, shot down in error by an Italian pilot. In the poem Yeats takes on the voice of

14   Samuel Beckett, *Watt* (London: Faber and Faber, 2009. Orig. Paris: Olympia Press, 1953), 218.

the airman and identifies with the heroic individualism of the man, rather than with the politics and pressures of the time. For this *Irish* airman is fighting in a British imperial war but he has become involved not for any other reason than a 'lonely impulse of delight'. The air man is a swan, in a sense, 'among the clouds.'[15] (Those clouds again.)

In his imagined mind, anticipating his own death, as so many hundreds of thousands of soldiers had done during the brutal industrialised killing of First World War, Yeats's poem shifts the focus away from the bloody reality of war and seizes upon the posthumous recognition of the pilot's own very private death, an existential challenge that has no bearing upon the ordinary lives of those men and women in the west of Ireland who he will (or has) left behind. 'An Irish Airman ...' is caught up just a little with the arguments of that time in Ireland about the rights and wrongs of Irish men and women fighting for the British state: 'Nor law, nor duty bade me fight, /Nor public men, nor cheering crowds.'[16] On 'balance', Yeats implies, the only reason for such likely sacrifice is 'delight'. And it is a justification when one compares the heroic image of the airman as he pierces the clouds to meet his own 'fate', with the portrait of the two contemporary women friends of Yeats, Eva Gore-Booth and her sister, Constance.

For having both been young beauties when Yeats first met them in 1894/1895, in their family home of Lissadell in County Sligo ('that old Georgian mansion'), now towards *his* old age, Yeats recalls 'That table and the talk of youth' and compares their shared youth, which has gone, with the women's fate. Eva had died in her mid-50s after much illness and a life dedicated to politics and a sense of duty to those less fortunate than herself: 'Some vague Utopia' he calls this commitment that ends in the prematurely aged figure of Eva: '... withered old and skeleton-gaunt, / An image of such politics.'[17]

While Eva's slightly older sister, Constance, died a year after her, she too represents to Yeats an unfulfilled life. Having been sentenced to death for her military role in the 1916 Rising (and subsequently pardoned but

15 Yeats, 'An Irish Airman Foresees his Death', 184.
16 Yeats, 'An Irish Airman Foresees his Death', 184.
17 Yeats, 'In Memory of Eva Gore-Booth and Con Markiewicz', 283–284.

imprisoned in England), Constance, 'drags out lonely years/ Conspiring among the ignorant.' Actually she was the first ever woman MP elected to Westminster (though she never took up her seat) and was also the first woman Minister in a European parliament! But from their early exotic promise – 'Two girls in silk kimonos, both/Beautiful, one a gazelle' – to 'lonely years' and 'skeleton-gaunt', Yeats's commemoration of both women who have now gone ('now you know it all') sees them as emblems of a way of life that is itself 'over', for 'The innocent and the beautiful/Have no enemy but time'. While neither 'innocent' nor 'beautiful', the same can be said for Yeats. So that the summerhouse (or 'gazebo') which has been a picture in his mind of a proper relaxed way of life, at ease with itself and the orderly world of the big house, it in turn appears fated; a foolish thing that even sounds foolish – ga'-ze'-bo.

'In Memory …' is an elegy of sorts, but the refrain of beauty and the acknowledgement that both girls are 'Dear shadows' takes the sting of loss away in the concluding lines of a selfless ritual of Japanese-like praise to follow on from the Japanese inflected costume of kimonos: 'They convicted us of guilt;/Bid me strike a match and blow.' So the whole poem goes up in flames.

By the end of his own time, Yeats wanted his poems to become as expressive to future generations as they had been during his working life. In the final sections of 'Under Ben Bulben' he takes his reader back to the beginning; to his imaginative home. The poem-parts – the six sections – move in and out of different kinds of register and rhetoric. The pacey poetic clip of section five is ballad-like; 'recitable' as a song should be and it is full of admonition and instruction, looking backwards and forwards as all commemoration is meant to do. 'Cast your mind on other days/ That we in coming days may be/ Still the indomitable Irishry.'[18]

The tablet which adorns the entire poem, in section VI, is closely linked with Yeats's ongoing sense of self-dramatisation, except that here the self, which is being dramatised, is his own death and his own lasting legacy. The language of this eight-line part, along with the three lines of epigraph, is as simple and direct as a child's story, while the images scan all

18   Yeats, 'Under Ben Bulben', 375.

the way back to where Yeats's real poetry started, in the Sligo countryside. As previously noted, the stone is here too, limestone, but the sense of his own self becomes at one with the very place his imagination had drawn upon from that young man in London dreaming about Innisfree: 'bare Ben Bulben's head' where 'Yeats is laid'. The poet had become his mythology. For church and ancient cross stand out in cinematic clarity as the reader's eye homes in on the written (*italicised* for emphasis) words of commemoration: '*Cast a cold eye/ On life, on death,/ Horseman, pass by!*'[19]

Within the year Yeats had gone. The 'ancestor'[20] Yeats refers to is in a long line of ancestors to whom he had attached himself and his poetry along with the self-commemoration we noticed earlier in 'To be carved on a stone at Thoor Ballylee'. Yeats's poems look back to look forward. 'Since I first made my count', ' But now', 'Could we turn the years again', 'When, young and beautiful/She rode to harriers', 'But O that I were young again', 'recall/That table and talk of youth', 'in coming days'. This is not a complacent nostalgia though. It is important to see just how much of Yeats's poetry is actually a dramatic form of interrogation, calmly asking questions of his readers; sometimes playfully, sometimes balefully, sometimes haughtily; sometimes poignantly; sometimes lustily. He is an argumentative poet bent upon unsettling his reader:

> Among what rushes will they build,
> By what lake's edge or pool
> Delight men's eyes when I awake some day
> To find they have flown away?[21]

Questions abound in Yeats. Questions open 'September 1913' and the poem contains two further questions. There are five questions asked in 'Easter 1916'; a question opens 'Politics' and concludes 'The Second Coming'. Yeats continuously refers to ordinary speech and conversation. His poems are themselves full of 'talk' and when he gets going, his poems ramp up with 'high talk'; the rhetoric of his ancestor's sermons and the

---

19   Yeats, 'Under Ben Bulben', 376.
20   'An ancestor was rector there/ Long years ago', 375.
21   Yeats, 'The Wild Swans at Coole', 181.

love of language in Dublin's turn of the last century, an know-all inheritance of political debate and cultural discourse that James Joyce would satirise.

There is the landscape of the poems based around a fixed point of reference at the centre of his writing; a house, for instance, upon which the personal and visionary compass is drawn, or like the falconer, or even the dreaded 'slouching beast' as 'all about it/Reel shadows of the indignant desert birds'. There are no deserts in Ireland, Yeats had to make them up in a Shelleyan wonder, although he knew full well that, like Swift, after a long and mighty career, he had himself 'sailed into his rest'. But Yeats's influence would far outlast his death and the allure of his achievement survives and played a crucial role in the formation of several poets of the second half of the twentieth century who went on to establish international reputations to whom I will now turn.

II

There is a very interesting anecdote recounted in Richard Murphy's memoir, *The Kick: A Life among Writers* about Ted Hughes and Sylvia Plath visiting him in Cleggan, Co. Galway in 1962. Murphy was playing host and on the day after they arrived, he recalls 'there was a forecast of rain and south-east winds, making a passage to the island undesirable. So I took them to Yeats's Tower at Ballylee and Lady Gregory's Coole Park':

> … I showed them the copper beech tree in the Pleasure Ground. Sylvia urged Ted to climb a spiked iron fence that protected the tree, and to carve his initials beside those of Yeats. She said he deserved to be in that company more than some of the Irish writers – J. M. Synge, AE, George Bernard Shaw – who had made their now almost illegible mark. But the spikes were too sharp for him to climb over. [22]

And then to The Tower, at Ballylee: '[T]hey noticed a moss-coated apple tree, planted in the time of Yeats, bearing a heavy crop of bright red

22   Richard Murphy, *The Kick: A Life among Writers* (London: Granta, 2003), 222.

cookers. Ted and Sylvia both insisted they we should steal them. I pro-
tested … . My objections were brushed aside. I asked Ted "Why are you
doing this?" Standing with his back to the grey limestone wall of the
Tower he spoke in a voice of quiet intensity: "When you come to a place
like this you have to violate it." '[23]

Why Hughes felt the need to 'violate' 'a place like this' is anyone's
guess, while Sylvia Plath's urging him 'to carve his initials beside those of
Yeats' probably says more about Sylvia's state of mind (her suicide took
place the following year) than anything else. Like that fateful Hughes/Plath
pilgrimage, getting close to Yeats's name and territory has proven to be a
rite of passage for many poets over very many years both before and since.

Various visiting poets such as John Berryman, Theodore Roethke and
R. S. Thomas had come in search of the man's genius, both its legacy but
also to in some way draw inspiration from Yeats's imaginative powerhouse
and terrain. For those who resided – if only briefly – under Yeats's contemporary spell, there was also a complex sense of his stature worldwide
alongside frustration and often mockery of the great man's persona. If T. S.
Eliot recalled his meeting with affection: 'I met him once', he remarks to
Richard Murphy, 'when I was young and he was quite old and famous.
What impressed me most was his courtesy; Yeats treated me as an equal.'[24]

Samuel Beckett also met Yeats once but had a somewhat different
experience, if we accept the word of Deirdre Bair, who commented that
the encounter took place 'only once, during a brief encounter in Killiney,
where [Beckett] was disgusted with the way W. B. Yeats simpered over his
wife and made an inordinate fuss with the children'.[25]

However, Beckett would return to Yeats's work throughout his own
plays – naming one late piece '… but the clouds …' after lines from Yeats's
poem 'The Tower'. And as recounted in Anne Atik's *How It Was: A Memoir
of Samuel Beckett*, Beckett's unwavering admiration for Yeats's poems lasted

23   Murphy, *The Kick*, 223.
24   Murphy, 216.
25   Deirdre Bair, *Samuel Beckett: A Biography* (London: Picador, 1980), 121.
       For a fuller treatment of Beckett's understanding of Yeats, see Gerald
     Dawe, 'Hearing Things', *The Wrong County: Essays on Modern Irish Writing*
     (Newbridge: Irish Academic Press, 2018), 1–16.

into his own old age when he would recite Yeats's verse from memory. Yeats's 'The Tower' was particularly significant for him. When A. J. ('Con') Leventhal, one of Beckett's dearest friends, died in October 1979, Beckett turned to the Yeats poem for comfort.[26]

In his ongoing darts at Yeats and the legacy of the Yeatsian Celtic Revival or Twilight, Patrick Kavanagh altered course between biting satire and a sense of the poetic mastery of form which Yeats displayed throughout his long, productive and highly successful life:

> All the Paddies having fun
> Since Yeats handed in his gun.
> Every man completely blind
> To the truth about his mind.[27]

From the opening of his satire 'The Paddiad or: the Devil as a Patron of Irish Letters', Kavanagh produced a nightmarish scenario of post-Yeatsian fallout. The poem, originally published in 1949, concluded his last magnificent single volume, *Come Dance with Kitty Stobling* (1960). The setting of a pub to the non-boozer Yeats stretches the point of difference but there is a flintiness here that the Yeats of 'September 1913' or 'Crazy Jane' might have understood and even applauded:

> 'A great renaissance is under way'
> You can hear the devil say
> As into our pub comes a new arrival,
> A man who looks the conventional devil:
> This is Paddy Conscience, this
> Is Stephen Dedalus.
> This is Yeats who ranted to
> Knave and fool before he knew,
> This is Sean O'Casey saying,
> Fare thee well to Innishfallen.[28]

---

26 Anne Atik, *How It Was: A Memoir of Samuel Beckett* (London: Thames and Hudson, 2001), 124.
27 Patrick Kavanagh, 'The Paddiad', *Collected Poems* (London: Allen Lane, 2004), 150–151.
28 Kavanagh, 'The Paddiad', 152.

'Paddy Conscience', an identity-kit of the good and the bad – gets a rough time of it in 'The Paddiad', 'losing his latest body, /Dead in Paris':

> Shocking news.
> I much admired all his views.
> A man of genius, generous, kind,
> Not a destructive idea in his mind.
> My dearest friend! Let's do him proud.
> Our wives will make a green silk shroud
> To weave him in. The Emerald Isle
> Must bury him in tourist style.[29]

Little remorse here for intemperate speech, that's for sure. Kavanagh's clearing out of the Twilighters and their hangers-on and his railing here against the heavily inflected parody of the Yeats-inspired beliefs are cast aside from the outset in a note prefacing 'The Paddiad' when it was republished in *Come Dance with Kitty Stobling*:

> This satire is based on the sad notion with which my youth was infected that Ireland was a spiritual entity. I had a good deal to do with putting an end to this foolishness, for as soon as I found out I reported the news widely. It is now only propagated by the BBC in England and in the Bronx in New York and the Departments of Irish literature at Princeton, Yale, Harvard and New York universities.
>
> I have included this satire but wish to warn the reader that it is based on the above-mentioned false and ridiculous premises.[30]

A bold statement indeed, given the rising tide of piety that surrounded the idea of 'Ireland' when Kavanagh was trying to eke out with great difficulty a writer's life in the capital.

Everywhere one casts an eye on Irish poetry Yeats's influence remains central and in one way or another defining. Louis MacNeice's early study of his compatriot, *The Poetry of W. B. Yeats* [31] was, according to Terence Brown's biography of Yeats, for the 'young Ulster-born poet of Anglo-Irish stock' completing the book 'after the outbreak of hostilities', a way to assess

29　Kavanagh, 155.
30　Reprinted in Kavanagh, *Collected Poems*, 276.
31　Louis MacNeice, *The Poetry of W B Yeats* (London: Faber and Faber, 1941).

Yeats, first and foremost, but also a way of 'sorting out a personal muddle about his [MacNeice's] country.'[32] Brown continues: 'For Ireland has chosen neutrality in the world war (a stance Yeats's last poem "The Black Tower" can be seen to advise)… as a poet and reader of poetry [MacNeice] was also keen to characterise Yeats' legacy to practitioners, while as a poet/a critic and man he understood that Yeats presented a test case of a very special kind on the question of belief in poetry and life.'[33]

In another 'last' poem, 'Man and the Echo' (1938), Yeats worries over his life and questions whether or not an early play of his, *Cathleen ni Houlihan* (1902) was morally culpable in encouraging the violence of 1916 and the subsequent decade of turbulence in Irish history:

> I lie awake night after night
> And never get the answers right.
> Did that play of mine send out
> Certain men the English shot?[34]

A question which would indeed rumble down the decades until Paul Muldoon, in his sequence, '7, Middagh Street' answered back quite resoundingly:

> As for his [Yeats's] crass, rhetorical
> Posturing, 'Did that play of mine
> Send out certain men (*certain* men?)
>
> the English shot …?'
> the answer is 'Certainly not'.
>
> If Yeats had saved his pencil-lead
> would certain men have stayed in bed?[35]

And off we go again: Yeats with all the leading questions. One can see and hear shadows and shades of Yeats's presence in Irish poetry. It is full of echoes and soundings, scratchings out, allusions and elisions, borrowings

32   Terence Brown, *The Life of W. B. Yeats* (Oxford: Blackwell Publishers, 1999), 378.
33   Brown, *The Life of W. B. Yeats*, 378.
34   Yeats, *The Poems*, 392.
35   Paul Muldoon, *Meeting the British* (London: Faber and Faber, 1987), 39.

and disavowals, from the critical responses of his younger contemporaries who knew him, such as Thomas MacGreevy, to those heavily indebted to him such as F. R. Higgins and those like Austin Clarke who turned to Yeats's epical strain of dramatic verse.

It was as a young boy growing up in New York that Patrick Joseph O'Connor first heard his mother reading Yeats's poems to him and asking him to promise that he would return home to Ireland. O'Connor did intend return and turned himself in the poet Padraic Fiacc, his first poems clearly indebted to Yeats and his mentor Padraic Colum. Yeats's talismanic presence, however, resurfaces in the poems of Fiacc's most identified with the Northern Troubles such as his second volume, *Odour of Blood* (1973) which takes its title from Yeats's play *The Resurrection* (1931):

> Odour of blood when Christ was slain
> Made all Platonic tolerance vain
> And vain all Doric discipline.[36]

Yeats has been an impulse within Irish poetry, central to its potency and global reach. Eavan Boland's *W. B. Yeats and His World* (1971), a collaboration with Micheal Mac Liammóir, published in the famous Thames and Hudson series, is one in a long line of contemporary Irish poets and writers' personal and critical engagement with Yeats's life and writing. From the deconstructing essays of Seamus Deane to W. J. McCormack's contentious reading of Yeats's politics in *Blood Kindred: W. B. Yeats, The Life, The Death, The Politics* (2005), Nicholas Grene's reassertion of *Yeats's Poetic Codes* (2008) to Roy Foster's magisterial *W. B. Yeats: A Life* and subsequent Yeats-related material he has published – historians, scholars and critics from Ireland remain focused on Yeats's legacy.

Edna Longley's study *Yeats and Modern Poetry* (2013) brings to Yeats a much-needed realignment with his abiding influence on poetry in English. And of course Yeats's place in the achievement of fellow Irish poets is unmistakable. In choosing a selection of Yeats's poetry for the *Field Day Anthology of Irish Writing* (1990), in his essays and in his edition of Yeats's poetry,

---

36 'The Resurrection', *The Collected Works of W. B. Yeats: Vol II The Plays*, edited by David R. Clark and Rosalind E. Clark (Basingstoke: Palgrave, 2001), 492.

Seamus Heaney was clear about what makes Yeats matter so much 'When all the objections have been lodged, Yeats's work survives as a purely motivated, greatly active power for good …. Yeats's incitements to generous self-transcendence, his fostering of all that is unconstrained and enjoys full scope, contribute greatly to the value of his work.'[37]

But I will conclude with the words of another Irish poet, Derek Mahon, whose style of address, while seemingly distinctly un-Yeatsian at times, captures in essence the attraction of Yeats's poetry to the young and eager poet Mahon had once been, turning to Yeats for the first time as he recalls in this retrospective of his student days at Trinity College: 'We came to think of him as unassailable where the poetry itself was concerned, if open to serious question in matters of politics and philosophy … he seemed to have spirited himself away until only the work remained, a monument of its own magnificence.'[38]

37   Seamus Heaney, *W. B. Yeats: Poet to Poet* (London: Faber and Faber, 2004), xxiv–xxv.
38   Derek Mahon 'Yeats and the Lights of Dublin', *Selected Prose* (Oldcastle: The Gallery Press, 2012), 74–75.

CHAPTER 3

Self-Portraits: Patrick Kavanagh

What follows is closer to a reading than to a formal lecture because I am going to explore how poets who established their reputations after Kavanagh first made contact with him and what their impressions were of the poet, his example and influence. I could choose from any number of Irish poets but have selected five examples in an effort to be concise and representative before focusing on Kavanagh's legacy; a kind of Kavanaghesque thing to do since so often in his poems he had his eye on the future, even though he seemed to be preoccupied with the past.

The five examples I am going to read from are in order – Seamus Heaney, Thomas Kilroy, Eavan Boland, Michael Longley and Paul Durcan before concluding with a name that might not be so familiar but will be: Jacki Mc Carrick, a playwright and fiction-writer, whose fascinating essay on Kavanagh as 'a sculptor-poet' compares him with Barbara Hepworth, among other sculptors whom, she writes, 'hail from Yorkshire: Hepworth, Moore and [Richard] Long … a territory not in parts dissimilar to Monaghan/ North Louth.'[1]

'I want to keep the focus personal', Heaney writes in his essay 'The Placeless Heaven', 'and look at what Kavanagh has meant to one reader, over a period of a couple of decades'.[2] His sense of Kavanagh deserves to be quoted in full but this early portrait is revealing not just of Kavanagh's importance but of how Heaney would use that authority to 'dwell without

---

1   Jacqueline Mc Carrick, 'A New Thing Breathing: The Landscape Art of Patrick Kavanagh', M. Phil in Irish Writing paper (Trinity College Dublin, April 2004), 7.

2   Seamus Heaney 'The Placeless Heaven: Another Look at Kavanagh', *Finders Keepers Selected Prose 1971–2001* (London: Faber and Faber, 2002), 134–144. Heaney's original 'look' was 'The Poetry of Patrick Kavanagh: From Monaghan to the Grand Canal' published in Douglas Dunn (ed.), *Two Decades of Irish Writing, A Critical Survey* (Cheadle, Cheshire: Carcanet Press, 1975), 105–117.

cultural anxiety among the usual landmarks of your life'. 'Kavanagh's genius', Heaney wrote in 1985, 'had achieved singlehandedly what I and my grammar-schooled, arts-degreed generation were badly in need of – a poetry that linked the small-farm life which had produced us to the slim-volume world we were not supposed to be fit for. He brought us back to what we came from. So it was natural that, to begin with, we overvalued the subject matter of the poetry at the expense of its salutary spirit. In the 1960s I was still susceptible to the pathos and familiarity of Kavanagh's poetry than I was alert to the liberation and subversiveness of its manner.'

A few years earlier in a lecture that was subsequently published as 'The Irish Writer: Self and Society, 1950–80', Thomas Kilroy describes the contradictions in Kavanagh's public personae. He was, 'firstly … a great comic writer and, secondly … he is the last in a rich, native rural tradition in which the poetic gift confers a status in the community, the status of waspish eccentricity'.[3] Drawing out the implications of this 'status' Kilroy's representation of Kavanagh in his Dublin years is both shocking and memorable: 'He stalks through the fifties like some *cainteoir* out of the Gaelic past with that sartorial stamp, the swinging coat, the dipped, brooding hat, the notorious cough and splutter, arms akimbo, knotted like an embrace that has lost or crushed its loved object.'[4]

The significance of this dramatic presentation of self, this mask, is left unexamined for, according to Kilroy's conclusion, it 'will be the business of the biographer to analyse the kind of distortions of selfhood which Kavanagh affected in his role as poet and to question the kind of society which impelled him, often with great cruelty and delight in the histrionics, towards the worst caricaturing, a perverse form of self-satisfaction on the part of society itself'.[5]

It is interesting to note how both Heaney and Kilroy, who come from rural Ireland (Heaney from Derry, Kilroy from Kilkenny) respond to the

---

3   Thomas Kilroy 'The Irish Writer: Self and Society, 1950–1980', *Literature and the Changing Ireland*, edited by Peter Connolly (Gerrards Cross: Colin Smythe, 1982), 175–187.

4   Kilroy, 'The Irish Writer', 186.

5   Kilroy, 186.

'role' Kavanagh played as a man of his background and time into the emerging 'new' Ireland.

In 'Turning Away', a chapter in her memoir-study *Object Lessons*, Eavan Boland recounts meeting Kavanagh 'in a café at the end of Grafton Street in Dublin. It was in the middle sixties. He was within two years or so of his death.'[6] Boland would have been in her early 20s at this time, recently graduated from Trinity College, and publishing her own poems.

In her memoir Kavanagh emerges with all his contradictions in place. 'His style of speech was shy and apocalyptic. He had a distinctive register of amazement, impatience and dismissal. He spoke with real irritation about certain characters, "poetasters", as he would have called them.'[7]

But the significance of the meeting, registered thirty or so years later, is not lost in Boland's recollection. On the contrary, it is the point. 'I had touched something which would return to me later: an example of dissidence. Kavanagh was a countryman; I was a woman. Neither of those circumstances had much meaning for the other. But I had seen the witness of someone who had used the occasion of his life to rebuff the expectations and preconceptions of the Irish poem. I would remember it.'[8]

As indeed she does when recalling Kavanagh's affection for the canal way near his Dublin flat: 'There was nothing particularly beautiful about the spot .... It was a noisy inch of city, shadowed by poplars and intruded on by passersby. He had been a sick man then, disillusioned and estranged. And with his foot on that inch, he had written a visionary sonnet. I never passed the canal at that point without thinking of it. *O commemorate me where there is water.* There was something so downright and local about the poem that it opened out, for the first time, the idea of place as something language could claim even if ownership had been denied.'[9]

Boland's slightly older Trinity College contemporary Michael Longley in 'A Jovial Hullaballoo', looks back to his first contact with Kavanagh. 'For my 21st birthday a friend gave me Kavanagh's *Come Dance with Kitty*

---

6 Eavan Boland, *Object Lessons: The Life of the Woman and the Poet in Our Time* (London: Vintage 1996), 98.
7 Boland, *Object Lessons*, 98–99.
8 Boland, 99–100.
9 Boland, 102.

Stobling' but a slight hint of impatience, continues: 'I have never thought in Irish dynastic terms and I don't see myself or my poetic colleagues in some kind of Irish succession. I dislike literary ancestor worship.'[10] And with this caveat firmly in mind Longley makes the telling point that 'if I had to choose two Irish poetic uncles, they would be Louis MacNeice and Patrick Kavanagh – the Kavanagh who wrote this immaculate lyric: "Consider the grass growing/ As it grew last year and the year before,/ Cool about the ankles like summer rivers /When we walked on a May evening through the meadows/To watch the mare that was going to foal." '

In 'The Drumshambo Hustler: A celebration of Van Morrison'[11] Paul Durcan sounds a Kavanagh-like warning about 'literary people': 'that whole mafia of literary wheeler-dealers comprising James Bonds academics, Ayatollah publishers, hysterical columnists, club critics, who bestride the one vast literary bidet on the slopes of Parnassus: there they squat all year round, hooded fossils, self-regarding, satisfied, oblivious, brooding, conspiring.' Durcan makes the important connection between 'Both Northerners – solid ground boys' and in a wonderful riff of his own pays homage to Morrison and 'that great other Irish jazzman of the twentieth century', Kavanagh. As parallel artists each in their own right Durcan nominates both 'top of my list in a new curriculum' for the Leaving Certificate Poetry course. 'Van Morrison's rendition of Patrick Kavanagh's "On Raglan Road" is fitting because it brings together the two finest poets in Ireland in my lifetime. No other poets – writing either in verse or in music – have come within a Honda's roar of Kavanagh and Morrison.' True to his word, Durcan's early poem 'November 30, 1967' (dedicated to Katherine, Kavanagh's wife) commemorates his passing with spoken words he hears in Mooney's pub from 'an old Northsider': 'He was pure straight, God rest him, not like us.'[12] And in the short lyric 'They Say the

10   Michael Longley, 'A Jovial Hullaballoo', *One Wide Expanse: Writing from the Ireland Chair of Poetry* (Dublin: University College Dublin Press, 2015), 6.
11   Paul Durcan, 'The Drumshambo Hustler: A celebration of Van Morrison', *Magill*, May 1988, 56–57.
12   Paul Durcan, 'November 30, 1967', *A Snail in My Prime: New and Selected Poems* (London: The Harvill Press / Belfast: Blackstaff Press, 1993), 3.

Butterfly is the Hardest Stroke' Durcan reminds his reader of the psychic barriers Kavanagh has broken through and in whose company he belongs:

> I have not "read"
> David Gascoyne, James Joyce, or Patrick Kavanagh:
> I believe in them.
> Of the song of him with the world in his care
> I am content to know the air.[13]

Terence Brown in 'After the Revival: O'Faolain and Kavanagh' quotes Kavanagh's 'Innocence'[14] as an example of his 'surest achievement'. 'In moments of such charged lyric assurance [Kavanagh] exhibits the possibility of an Irish art, that grounded in ordinary Irish reality excites "the moment of hope". Irish life transcends for an exemplary moment the problem of adequacy.' While praising this 'achievement in lyric art' Brown reflects that 'even at its most ecstatic and intense' the poem suggests 'a triumph of quietism.' For Jacqueline McCarrick, however, 'quietism' might be not quite the right word to describe Kavanagh's visual world.

In a fresh reading of his verse, McCarrick connects Kavanagh's imagination with the work of sculptors. 'Clay, stones, the bog, rocks, potatoes, buckets, barrels, seeds, markets, wheels, the black hills, the rough-tongued people, the railways and travelling, travelling and returning, the industrious ways of the rural – these all comprise, amongst much else, Kavanagh's early references and source materials. For a self-taught artist in the borderlands in the [19]20s and 30s to have grasped the essentially modern concept of taking those materials most immediately at hand, otherwise ugly, rough and banal materials, to create personal and intimate art, is astonishing.'[15]

The power of the word 'astonishing' should not pass the reader by because, as McCarrick points out, Kavanagh in his poems 'can only be imagined actively, physically "poem-making"; his hands come into view; the poem seems dug-up and shaped. In the language and imagery used in

13   Paul Durcan, 'They Say the Butterfly is the Hardest Stroke', *A Snail in My Prime*, 7.
14   Terence Brown, 'After the Revival: O'Faolain and Kavanagh', *Ireland's Literature: Selected Essays* (Dublin: Lilliput Press, 1988), 114–115.
15   Jacqueline McCarrick, 'A New Thing Breathing: The Landscape Art of Patrick Kavanagh', 4.

Kavanagh's early work … the sculptor-poet is clearly present. The material is hewn, objectified, and physically present on the page, sometimes as if created with a plough or scythe. The choice to use available "banal" material, places Kavanagh alongside other contemporaneous modernist artists: Jean Arp, Barbara Hepworth, Henry Moore, Ben Nicholson and Naum Gabo of the Constructivists – all sought a greater degree of intimacy with simple, plain and common material, and all sought to find the "essence" of these, via retaining elements of setting and landscape.'[16]

As I have tried to show here, Kavanagh's influence is long-lasting and diverse. While the future of his legacy in Ireland seems secure the question needs to be asked – should we not be going further to register internationally both in the publication of his work, but also in the promotion of his achievement? We have *Tarry Flynn*, *The Green Fool*, *Collected Poems* and *Selected Poems*, all in Penguin editions. Why not convert these, as Penguin has done in the case of Yeats and Joyce, into a series 'The Penguin Kavanagh', and include along the way editions of his journalism; for instance, *A Poet's Country: Selected Prose* (2003) is already available in a scholarly edition edited by Antoinette Quinn. But also perhaps produce a commemorative edition of *Self-Portrait*, with images from the original 'Self-Portrait' series broadcast by Telefís Eireann, as it was then.

Would it not be a substantial contribution to 'Kavanagh Studies' if present-day RTÉ were to remaster the original portrait along with the televised documentary on Kavanagh in 'The Writers' series the national station broadcast on 10 October 1966 shortly before Kavanagh's death on 30 November 1967?

A double CD distributed through the school system in Ireland and globally through the Department of Foreign Affairs and Ireland embassies would be timely and appropriate and bring attention to the country and countryside in a fashion not dissimilar from the magnificent W. B. Yeats exhibition at the National Library. Beckett at 100 celebrations, the annual 'Joycefest' and other more recent commemorations, including the 'Listen Now Again' Seamus Heaney exhibition in the Bank of Ireland Cultural and Heritage Centre in Dublin.

16   McCarrick, 'A New Thing Breathing', 13.

Kavanagh is the less deceived of modern Irish writers and he deserves the full literary and cultural recognition that twenty-first Ireland can muster because in his life's struggles, in his hard-won creativity and artistic achievement, we are all in his debt, now more than ever – to his personal legacy and witness, to his continuing influence as poet, primarily, but also as essayist, commentator, fiction writer and memorialist. It is Patrick Kavanagh the writer who is magnificent, not 'the character' into which he was turned. As he put it himself in the challengingly delayed aftermath of his great poem 'I Had a Future':

> Show me the stretcher-bed I slept on
> In a room on Drumcondra Road.
> Let John Betjeman call for me in a car.
>
> It is summer and the eerie beat
> Of madness in Europe trembles the
> Wings of the butterflies along the canal.
>
> O I had a future

CHAPTER 4

The Cage: John Montague

Generally speaking, in the life of any significant writer, it is likely that there is at least one critical moment or influence in their early experiences that propelled them to writing and from this source their writing springs. This is a need to express themselves not for commercial gain, not to be recognised, for 'fame', though elements of these might come into play. What I mean is something much more necessary and deepseated. The writers I have in mind are those – more often than not, poets – whose writing is an integral part of their identity as individuals; whose 'self' is defined by the fact that they relate to the world through the prism of their imaginative reconstruction of things they experience, or witness, or come to terms with via their writing.

Such writers, it can be argued, understand the world, first and foremost, only *through* the writing; their poems or plays make sense of reality, make the necessary adjustments possible and act as consolations, compensations, rationale, experiments, for whatever it is they have gone through as individuals, either in childhood or later on. Love lost, for instance, is a great romantic version, or the denial of personal freedom in a repressive society – one thinks of poets during the Soviet Union – or the feelings of having missed out, been denied something, frustration with the mores and cultural stereotypes of a culture, such as our own, which Patrick Kavanagh railed against in the 1940s until his death in 1967. These feelings and experiences become understood and dramatised in the very act of writing.

So the history of an individual poet's work is both a personal history of actual events – Yeats writing about Easter 1916 for instance – and of real experiences – Kavanagh writing about life on a small farm on the border of northern and southern Ireland. But also the rendering of these transitory events and experiences into a form of stabilised literary art – the poem itself.

In Ireland we have a long tradition of poetry-making that sees in Irish history and the Irish landscape a code through which personal views are inscribed and read. Yeats's 'The Lake Isle of Innisfree' – to call on one very obvious example – is a poem about an island called Heather Island, situated in Lough Gill, in Sligo; but it is also a song about emigration. Patrick Kavanagh's 'Shancoduff' is about a range of hills in Monaghan but it is also about the poet's conflicting understanding that he needs to leave them in order to realise his 'self', or so he thinks, though Kavanagh would later question in his poems this very decision.

John Montague's poetry – as well as much that he has written as an essayist, translator and fiction writer – is based around this divided self and of how an early and irrevocable experience of family life influenced him greatly and largely determined the creative paths he would follow as a poet. This is the journey which began as far back as 1929 when John Montague was born in Brooklyn, New York, the son of two Irish emigrants who had moved to the United States in a generational sweep of migration that took place from Northern Ireland in the late 1920s and early 1930s as a result of the rapid collapse of job opportunities.

As previously noted, another Northern poet, Padraic Fiacc,[1] whose parents came originally from Cavan and Belfast, and who also grew up in New York – had also, like Montague's parents, left Ireland as a result of the original Troubles since both fathers had been involved in the IRA during the years of 'The Troubles'. That world is the bedrock of Montague's imaginative life. We know too that as a small boy he was uprooted from his original American family home and returned as a 5 year old to his father's sisters in Garvaghey, County Tyrone in the 1930s.

The life he lived in Tyrone, discovering the countryside, the school he went to, the home life, the unfolding sense of in some way of his having being cast adrift, even when his mother returned to Ireland, leaving behind Montague's father, is the very stuff of the drama of his poetry.

---

1   Gerald Dawe, 'Odd Man Out', *Of War and War's Alarms* (Cork: Cork University Press, 2015), 126–140. Also Padraic Fiacc, *Ruined Pages: New Selected Poems* (Derry: Lagan Press, 2012).

For there is the bruising dichotomy between both worlds – the American and the Northern Irish – and how these rub against each other – in terms of expectations, social mores, the realities of Irish rural life in the early part of the mid-century – are set against the cosmopolitan possibilities of New York. And which is really only the beginning for the young Montague as he started to see differences that were playing themselves out in the newly established state of Northern Ireland by the late 1930s and into the period of 1940s and Second World War.

This is the defining experience I mentioned at the beginning. While it is often mentioned in passing in commentaries about John Montague's poetry, I see this early experience as being crucial to appreciating his work. For the separation became the imaginative drive to much of what Montague would produce as a poet since his first early steps to publication in Dublin and London of the 1950s and 1960s.

Montague tells the story of these times, and later of his return to the US, and the life he established for himself in Paris, Cork, and elsewhere in his two memoirs – *Company: A Chosen Life* (2001) and *The Pear is Ripe* (2007). There are also two other related titles that should be consulted regarding how contemporaries of Montague, poets and critics in the main, have responded to his life story and the poetry it has produced: *Hill Field: Poems & Memoirs for John Montague* (1989) and *Chosen Lights: Poets on Poems by John Montague* (2009).

Each of these titles helps to establish in greater detail the literary and political contexts within which to engage with what is unmistakably Montague's masterpiece – his *New Collected Poems* (2012) including poems from his earliest collections such as *Poisoned Lands* (1961), the epic poetic sequences, *The Rough Field* (1972) and *The Dead Kingdom* (1984) and the meditation on his own family history, 'In My Grandfather's Mansion' from *Speech Lessons* (2011), the title poem of which describes the trauma of his early efforts to overcome a debilitating speech impediment which remained with the poet to his death in 2016 aged 87.

It is simply not possible to portray *New Collected Poems* in any detail given the unfolding orchestration of the book, full of sequences and echoes, like a vast rich tapestry, and circling back on itself. Instead, I am going to look at some themes that recur in Montague's work over and over again, such as home, love, nature and history. Of these. the most telling and long-lasting to which Montague has returned over his extensive career, is 'home' and his sense of dislocation; dislocation in very many guises.

If there are key defining experiences that produce particular individual pathways in which distinctive thoughts and literary metaphors become in effect the hallmark of a poet's work through which they are known, the following extracts from his introduction to *The Figure in the Cave and Other Essays*, a volume of his selected essays reveals much.

> I was born in Brooklyn, St Catherine's Hospital, Bushwick Avenue, in 1929, the year of the Depression. I returned there in the mid-1980s at the insistence of a journalist from *Newsday*; I feared to find the usual run-down brownstone. To my astonishment there was more left of the neighbourhood than of Garvaghey [Co. Tyrone]
>
> … my two elder brothers were sent home to the small town where they had been born, resuming their Fintona lives after only a five-year-break in America. In Derry the children were shared out, and I went home with my aunt to become the last Montague, in the male line, to live in Garvaghey.[2]

This further quotation speaks for itself: 'It is like a fairy-tale, the little child who was sent away being received back with open arms. But while awed at the reappearance of this golden cradle to rock my dotage, I am grateful to have explored Ireland so intimately. Standing-stones and streams are not part of Brooklyn, nor are *cailleachs*. To judge by my contemporaries I would probably have been a writer, certainly a journalist, had I stayed in America. But who cut the long wound of poetry into my youth? Was it my mother who chose for her own good reasons to cast me off?'[3]

So this may be a good place to turn to Montague's poems by considering the connection he recounts between his father and the story told in 'The Cage: 'we/did not smile in/the shared complicity/of a dream, for when /weary Odysseus returns/ Telemachus should leave.'[4] Along with

---

2   John Montague, *The Figure in the Cave and Other Essays* (Dublin: Lilliput Press, 1989), 1–2.

3   Montague, *The Figure in the Cave*, 18.

4   John Montague, 'The Cage', *New Collected Poems* (Oldcastle: Gallery Press, 2012), 59. All quotations are taken from this collection.

the heart-breaking drama of 'The Locket' addressed to his mother, both poems present two sides of that early separation, the key, in my reading, to Montague's art. 'I never knew', the poet states, 'until you were gone,/ that around your neck,/ you wore an oval locket/ with an old picture in it, /of a child in Brooklyn.'[5]

Love, both physical and emotional, become one in 'The Same Gesture' ('it is what we always were – most nakedly are,'[6]) whereas the seeming 'nature' poem of 'The Trout', dedicated to fellow artist, the painter Barrie Cooke, captures the otherness of life and the shock the poet finds in experiencing, firstly, the sensuous life of the fish, and then registers the shock of his human control: 'I could count every stipple/ But still cast no shadow, until// The two palms crossed in a cage/ Under the lightly pulsing gills.'[7]

If Montague's poetry is literally full of creaturely lives, he has an extraordinary interest in and feeling for the physical nature of the Irish countryside. Wonderfully knowledgeable about different places throughout the length and breadth of the island, as I can testify from personal experience, Montague's poetry *knows* the countryside very well indeed. From city to village, pre-Christian to post-Christian, Ireland in Montague's poetry is a landscape that is first and foremost worked but is also reproduced, restored and recounted through the imagination of artists – with whom he has had a long life of collaborations – such as the painter Patrick Collins, to whom he dedicated 'Windharp': 'a hand ceaselessly /combing and stroking/ the landscape, till / the valley gleams / like the pile upon/ a mountain pony's coat.'[8]

Of this poem, Michael Longley remarked in *Chosen Lights*: 'Syllable and breathing-space interact with great refinement. We read these lines with bated breath and are drawn into an enraptured state of mind. Attentive, devout even, "Windharp" is a halting prayer, a broken spell. We are carried away and then brought down to earth. I look up to this celebrant of the Irish countryside, the precision of his descriptions. The spare music [.]'[9]

5   Montague, 'The Locket', 191.
6   Montague, 'The Same Gesture', 124.
7   Montague, 'The Trout', 225.
8   Montague, 'Windharp', 288.
9   Michael Longley, *Chosen Lights: Poets on Poems by John Montague*, edited by Peter Fallon (Oldcastle: Gallery Press, 2009), 71.

Michael Longley's final phrase ('spare music') summarises per-
fectly Montague's poetry. But perhaps the most jolting and troubling of
Montague's poems is 'A Welcoming Party'. Originally published in *Poisoned
Lands* in 1961 under a different title, the poem provides ample evidence of
how history and biography intersect in the workings of his poetry: 'From
nests of bodies like hatching eggs/ Flickered insectlike hands and legs/ And
rose an ululation, terrible, shy; / Children conjugating the verb "to die".'[10]

Brought back into his most intensely autobiographical volume *Time in
Armagh* (1993), 'A Welcoming Party' sets out to view his own upbringing
from the perspective of an older and much wiser man who has travelled
the world and seen how the greater picture can often be overlooked, or was
simply unavailable to the young schoolboy of the poem's final stanza: 'That
long dead Sunday in Armagh / I learnt one meaning of total war/ And
went home to my Christian school/ To belt a football through the air.' 'A
Welcoming Party' may well be one of the first, if not the first, 'Holocaust'
poem written by an Irish poet. It reveals the extent to which Montague
had tuned in to other frequencies than his own by the very early 1960s and
was seeing his Irish life and experience in terms of a much larger frame of
reference which he would explore as a poet and editor and translator for
decades to come.

Many writers have followed on from John Montague's steps back and
forward from New York to a home base in Ireland. He was in many ways
a forerunner of the Irish poet in the US university system. His transla-
tions from French and other European languages follow upon the work
of his older contemporary and friend Samuel Beckett, whom Montague
knew during his years in Paris. He certainly bridged the literary world *in*
Ireland between the at-times eviscerating 1950s, which Patrick Kavanagh
wrote about, and the international breakthrough of the 1960s 'group' of
Northern poets, including Derek Mahon.

While a generation of Irish writers who now live and work in the US,
among them, Eavan Boland and Paul Muldoon, recognise the extent to
which John Montague was transcribing emotional realities through his own
imagining of an Ireland he grew up in and which never left him, even

10   Montague, 'A Welcoming Party', 359.

though so much of that world had completely disappeared by the time his first collections of poetry started to appear in the 1960s and early 1970s. By which time, Derek Mahon's early collections would receive the kind of critical attention that a slightly older generation of poets in Ireland in many ways missed out on. It was a perception – this sense of neglect, or lack of recognition – which would shadow Montague's writerly life at a time when he could have been enjoying the acknowledgement of his younger contemporaries at home and abroad, including Mahon, Thomas McCarthy and the many others who contributed to *Chosen Lights: Poets on poems by John Montague*,[11] a book in honour of his 80th birthday in 2009.

11   Peter Fallon (ed.), *Chosen Lights; Poets on Poems by John Montague in Honour of His 80ᵗʰ Birthday* (Oldcastle: Gallery Press, 2009).

CHAPTER 5

Dreaming of Home: Derek Mahon

In Derek Mahon's poem 'The Chinese Restaurant in Portrush' what matters most are the three final words: as the 'proprietor of the Chinese restaurant/ Stands at the door as if the world were young' he 'whistles a little tune, dreaming of home.'[1] For 'dreaming of home' is what happens a lot in Derek Mahon's poetry; in *all* his collected work, the experience of 'dreaming' and 'home' take precedence over much else. Derek Mahon's 'home', the place in which he grew up, is, as it is for all of us, important; definitive and defining.

For Mahon home was Belfast, where he was born in 1941. Many of his early poems are linked directly with the city, its industrial past and its people. The continuing presence of that industrial landscape remains, like the inner décor of one's family home, primal to Mahon's imagination – the sounds and smells, the light and shade, the customs and lifestyles of what had been a thriving industrial city with a population (in 1971) of 600,000 people living and working in the great Belfast urban area. So it's hardly surprising to note that around the time when Mahon was publishing his first collections – *Night-Crossing* in 1968, *Lives* in 1972 – he should write in the introduction to an edition of modern Irish poetry which he selected in 1972, that whatever is meant by the phrase 'the Irish situation' 'the shipyards of Belfast are no less a part of it than a country town in the Gaeltacht'.

Home provides us with our earliest experiences, both inside the family, but outside: the way we speak, the geography of the place, the religion or religions, the understanding of community life, of the things people share – or reject – and the politics and assumptions that underpin life

---

1   Derek Mahon, 'The Chinese Restaurant in Portrush', *New Collected Poems* (Oldcastle: Gallery Press, 2011), 89. All quotations are taken from this collection.

and our cultural beliefs; these and more are found in the place (or places) we know as home.

But the idea of home and the condition of 'dreaming' of such a place, as the proprietor of the Chinese restaurant does in Portrush, County Derry – one of the most northerly points on the island of Ireland's coast – implies a detachment, of *not* being at home, but of thinking about it in an imagined wistful way, because he – 'the proprietor' – is not there in that home place, but removed, *far* removed. In thinking about how that Chinese man is thinking about home Mahon puts the reader in two places at the same time; indeed possibly *three*: we are 'in' Portrush, we are 'in' an imagined Chinese place, *and* we are in the mind of the Chinese proprietor who, like the poet, sees one place but imagines it to be another – his home. Or so Mahon implies. And it is this thoughtful meditation about home, this 'dreaming' that matters most to Mahon as a poet – not the sentiment, nor the landscape painting, but the *meaning* of home.

Indeed it is this shifting perspective, a kind of triangulation, which animates much of Mahon's poetry. He asks us to think about why and what it is about 'home' that makes it so important, that makes home *home* – familiarity, belonging, comfort, self-knowledge. In many of his poems these issues feature strongly as a common theme. For the bonds of home and the sense of local territory are often set alongside contrasting landscapes – between that which is different (and there are scales of difference) and that which is familiar.

Mahon's poems regularly journey between one place and another. The familiarity of home, literally the experience of family life, is examined with a cool objective eye. In other words, the rites and rituals associated with actual places – in which, for instance, ordinary family life 'happens' – are key to Mahon's poetic imagination. But what happens when home is no longer that, when such places fail or are no longer congenial?

Think of the effort Mahon's 'characters' take to make habitable *where* they live: the grandfather who has spent his life working in the famous Belfast shipyards is still not able to leave that industrial world behind him, so he rises 'up at six', even though he has no longer any work to go to 'But after dark/ You hear his great boots thumping in the hall/ And in he comes, as cute as they come. Each night/ His shrewd eyes bolt the door and set the clock/Against the future … .'[2]

There is the troubled figure of Bruce Ismay in 'After the Titanic' who hides from the tragic world of the *Titanic* disaster in a remote west of Ireland cottage, beseeching us, in Mahon's version of the tragedy, to understand *his* suffering and include him 'in our lamentations':

> 'I tell you/ I sank as far that night as any/ Hero. As I sat shivering on the dark water/ I turned to ice to hear my costly / Life go thundering down in a pandemonium of/ Prams, pianos, sideboards, winches, /Boilers bursting and shredded ragtime.'[3]

There is the figure in 'Day Trip to Donegal' who, returning from the stunning landscape of the north-west coastline, is unmanned and disorientated by the experience as he tries in 'vain' to settle back in the city suburbs that are 'sunk in a sleep no gale-force wind disturbs'[4]: a kind of deadly sleep.

The same can be said for 'Rathlin'[5] and its haunting difference which the poem's narrator briefly encounters on a visit to yet another remote northern island. Mahon's landscapes are often out of the way places, 'extremes' of isolation, remoteness, on the edge of things. And there is the shocking revelation at the heart of 'Antarctica', as Captain Oates, badly injured and casting about for a way of no longer burdening his 'family' of colleagues, 'leaves them reading' (as if in a Victorian parlour) and embraces his own death as a dreadfully necessary sacrifice: 'He takes leave of the earthly pantomime/ Quietly, knowing it is time to go.'[6] Even the mushrooms, long left to their own devices, call out in 'A Disused Shed in Co. Wexford' from their secret secreted places to those who visit them – 'To do something, to speak on their behalf'.

So it is important to recognise a significant pattern that these 'early' poems of Mahon's share – the act of journeying *to* and *from* some home

2   Mahon, 'Grandfather', 17.
3   Mahon, 'After the Titanic', 31
4   Mahon, 'Day Trip to Donegal', 26
5   Mahon, 'Rathlin', 98.
6   Mahon, 'Antarctica', 147.

place that leaves the poet (and his reader) in a state of restlessness; of not actually settling in any one place at all.

In fact, the poems focus in and out of place, as the narrators themselves are mostly visitors. While some of the poems are identified by proper nouns with definite places – Antarctica, Wexford, Rathlin, Kinsale, Donegal, Antrim – others allude to probable places – the Belfast of 'Grandfather' and 'Ecclesiastes' with its 'housing estates'. There is the 'starlit west' and 'bog' of 'As It Should Be'[7] and that 'lonely house behind the sea' in 'After the Titanic'.[8] Yet Mahon really is not so much interested in *describing* places. He is not a descriptive poet in the way that, for instance, Elizabeth Bishop is. His interest is much more philosophical, in questioning human reason and the reasons that drive us to want to be 'in' or find places to call home. So the relationship between the individual, his or her past, and the place they find themselves in and why, features strongly in many of Mahon's poems. Another way of saying this is that this relationship is the thread that links them together. One very clear example of this is 'Ecclesiastes' – an early poem of Mahon's but also one of his best-known, ironically remarks: 'and not feel called upon to understand and forgive/ but only to speak with a bleak afflatus and love the January rains when they / darken the dark doors and sink hard/ into the Antrim hills … .'[9]

Important to remember here that this poem, which has its source in the commandments of the Old Testament – a strongly Protestant feature of Mahon's Belfast upbringing – enjoys playing with language too – words such as 'afflatus' and 'credulous'. These untypical words are deliberately set alongside the everyday working-class world of the housing estates with 'their heavy washing', 'the dank /churches, the empty streets, /the shipyard silence, the tied-up swings' of what used to be a Sabbatarian Sunday in a Belfast long since transformed from those grim times I well remember.

But it is probably more important to note another crucial critical point about Mahon's use of English – how, along with that world of the everyday depicted in 'Ecclesiastes' – or the suburbs of 'Day Trip to Donegal', or the provincial feel of Portrush – Mahon often inserts a sense of the exotic – 'an

7   Mahon, 'As It Should Be', 49.
8   Mahon, 'After the Titanic', 31.
9   Mahon, 'Ecclesiastes', 36.

ideogram on sea-cloud' – which will de-familiarise and make strange whatever it is we as readers are looking at. Mahon often does this by using unusual, sometimes provocatively unfamiliar words and/or terms to jolt the reader out of too easy an identification with the poem at hand – 'pandemonium', 'oneiric', 'Cerulean', 'enzyme', 'foetor', 'mycologist', 'triffids' – words that need to be 'looked up' if only to better understand Mahon's playful sense of the value of the etymology of words. Words like 'pandemonium' which means the 'abode of all demons, hell, and is the capital of Hell in Milton's *Paradise Lost*; 'oneiric' is a Greek word meaning a dream, pertaining to dreams; Cerulean means sky-blue, the colour of a cloudless sky, which is almost a poem in itself; words like 'querulous' mean full of complaint; a perfect description for the cawing of rooks. And so on.

Mahon's later poems often extend these examples into comprehensive list of books, allusions to paintings and travelogues to exotic places such as India. So under the surface of the prosaic world of the everyday, Mahon sees and hears great differences to which these unusual words point, drawing the reader's attention to the specialness, the surprise, the bounty, the shock of another dreamy, or dreamier, reality beneath the strictly visible and known. I mentioned previously Elizabeth Bishop in contrast to Derek Mahon but another American poet, Wallace Stevens, comes to mind here as a useful comparison in his love of unusual, exotic language. In one of his most praised poems, 'A Disused Shed in Co. Wexford', the 'themes' I have been sketching in here converge: the notion of 'home', the idea of 'journey to and from a 'home' place, the role of 'dream' and of 'imagining', the redefining of what reality 'is' and how we access this other reality beyond or beneath the everyday world that we inhabit daily alongside Mahon's use of language – those 'unusual' key words and his form of dramatic address, how he uses 'speech' in his poems or gives voice to inanimate things.

It is necessary to start thinking about this great poem at the beginning – with the epigraph from George Seferis, the twentieth-century Greek poet. The line comes from the final (24th) part of Seferis's Homeric poem cycle, 'Mythistorema':

> Here end the works of the sea, the works of love
> Those who will some day live here where we end ---
> should the blood happen to darken in their memory and

                                        overflow ---
let them not forget us, the weak souls among the asphodels,
let them turn the heads of the victims towards Erebus:
We who had nothing will teach them peace.[10]

The reference to 'weak souls among the asphodels' comes from Homer's
Odyssey (Books XI and XXIV) where we are in the underworld, the land
of the dead, where 'easeful Hermes led them [the ghosts] down through
the ways of dankness. They passed the streams of Ocean, the White Rock,
the Gates of the Sun, and the Land of Dreams, and soon they came to the
field of asphodel, where the souls, the phantoms of the dead, have their
habitation.'[11]

The dedicatee of 'A Disused Shed in Co. Wexford' is J. G. Farrell, an
important Anglo-Irish novelist and dear friend of Mahon's in London
of the late 1960s and early 1970s. Farrell died tragically young in 1979 in
a fishing accident in west Cork. Mahon had shown his friend the poem
before it was published four years earlier and Farrell was flattered by the
dedication but the significance of the dedication would become part of
the personally charged elegiac quality of the poem itself. Mahon would
dedicate his subsequent collection, *The Hunt by Night* (1982) to Farrell. 'A
Disused Shed in Co. Wexford' picks up on elements in Farrell's early novel,
The Lung (published in 1965) – though there may also be slight echoes
of Farrell's novel *Troubles* (1970). This is the extract from *The Lung* – the
connection with Mahon's poem is unmistakeable:

> He remembered the door of a disused potting-shed he had once opened
> and the long, sickly white shoots racing each other interminably across
> the earth floor towards the minute bead of light from the keyhole. Tulips,
> or seed potatoes, or merely some anonymous weeks, it was impossible to
> tell. Perhaps by now one of them had reached the keyhole and, obstructing
> it, had condemned the other to death in darkness, only to expire itself in
> an unaccustomed blaze of sunshine.[12]

10   George Seferis, 'Mythistorema', *Collected Poems*, translated, edited and introduced
     by Edmund Keeley and Philip Sherrard (London: Anvil Press, 1982), 59.
11   Homer, *The Odyssey*, translated by Walter Shewring with an introduction by G. S.
     Kirk (Oxford/New York: Oxford University Press, 1980), 286.
12   J. G. Farrell, *The Lung* (London: Corgi Books, 1967 [orig.1965]), 27–28.

The poem is in essence an embodiment of all the strands and elements that I have been touching on here. Mahon's ability to bring in such diverse historical, narrative and visual material into one poem of six ten-lined stanzas makes this poem an appropriate point to reflect upon the artistic nature of his great achievement as a poet: 'They are begging us, you see, in their wordless way,/ To do something, to speak on their behalf/ Or at least not to close the door again./ Lost people of Treblinka and Pompeii!/ 'Save us, save us', they seem to say ... .'[13]

13   Mahon, 'A Disused Shed in Co. Wexford', 81.

CHAPTER 6

Our Words: Colette Bryce

*Omphalos, omphalos, omphalos … * The rhythm of the word that conjured up for [Seamus] Heaney the pump in his childhood yard – the Greek term for the centre of things – calls to mind the helicopters hovering over the cityscape of my childhood, a constant part of the soundtrack of growing up. The army would use the racket of propellers to drown out speeches at Free Derry Corner. So, in my mind, the blades are related to words, in opposition to our words, slicing up sentences in the wind.[1]

It is a mere coincidence that the Derry-born poet Colette Bryce is the concluding contributor to John Brown's *In the Chair: Interviews with poets from the North of Ireland,* published in 2002[2] and the first contributor to the third volume of *The Wake Forest Series of Irish Poetry,* edited by Conor O'Callaghan published eleven years later, in 2013.[3] Yet the period between tells its own story. By 2002 Bryce had published her first volume, *The Heel of Bernadette*[4] and in the following decade two further volumes appeared – *The Full Indian Rope Trick*[5] and *Self-Portrait in the Dark.*[6] And in the intervening period since, Bryce has gone on to secure an established name as one of the most important poets of her generation[7] with the publication of *The Whole & Rain-Domed*

---

1   Colette Bryce 'Omphalos: Returning to the troubles of a Northern Irish child-hood', *Poetry* (Vol. 205. No. 1) October 2014, 69–71 [69].

2   John Brown (ed.), *In the Chair: Interviews with Poets from the North of Ireland* (Cliffs of Moher: Salmon Press, 2002).

3   Conor O'Callaghan (ed.), *The Wake Forest Series of Irish Poetry* (Winston-Salem: Wake Forest, 2013).

4   Colette Bryce, *The Heel of Bernadette* (London: Picador 2000).

5   Colette Bryce, *The Full Indian Rope Trick* (London: Picador, 2004).

6   Colette Bryce, *Self Portrait in the Dark* (London: Picador, 2008).

7   A stellar generation it is too which includes, somewhat at random, and listing only Bryce's Irish contemporaries: David Wheatley, Sinead Morrissey, Catriona O'Reilly, John McAuliffe, Leontia Flynn and Nick Laird, all born in the early 1970s.

Universe,[8] *Selected Poems*[9] and the hugely impressive *The M Pages.*[10] Recognition has also come her way, for example, with the early Eric Gregory Award in 1995, National Poetry Competition in 2003 (UK), the prestigious Cholmondeley Award in 2010, the 2014 Ewart Biggs Award in memory of Seamus Heaney and in 2017 the Pigott Prize for Irish Poetry. She has also held important fellowships in universities in Britain and Ireland including Dundee, Newcastle-upon-Tyne and Trinity College Dublin as well as filling two important editorial positions with *Poetry London* and, more recently, *Poetry Ireland Review.*

This reading of Bryce's poetry is focused on the unfolding yet recurring presence of her home within an enclave of Derry city and the impact of her time both growing up there but also, crucially, her imaginative use of returning. How the physical intimacies of that home place align with a cultural sense of self is greatly influenced by two, key 'forces' – family and religion. How these critically play in and through the social and political crisis of Derry at such a traumatic time is also an important factor in what follows.

Born in 1970 Bryce's early upbringing and school-life took place during some of the worst events of the Troubles in Northern Ireland, some literally at her doorstep as she remarks[11]:

> I have memories of raids in the early hours where my mother would make the soldiers stack their rifles under the hall table before going through the house full of sleeping children. Barricades, rioting, burning vehicles, shootings and burnt out buildings were all part of the landscape. But this was normality.

When Bryce left Derry and moved to London in 1988 the crisis had another ten years to reach its apotheosis with the Good Friday Agreement of 1998, but I am interested in how these formative years surface in the mature poet's writing and her clear-sighted commentary on this period of her life. Given the extent and nature of the Derry world's sense of itself as

---

8   Colette Bryce, *The Whole & Rain-domed Universe* (London: Picador 2014).
9   Colette Bryce, *Selected Poems* (London: Picador 2017). Unless stated otherwise all poem quotations are taken from this publication in the interests of availability.
10   Colette Bryce, The *M Pages* (London: Picador 2020).
11   Brown, *In the Chair*, 311.

embattled and threatened, the (Catholic) community out of which Bryce came was best maintained in defiance of a repressive state and its sectarianised rule and order. That an authentic life is found and preserved within the reimagined family home and its intimate interconnections makes for a community of assumptions and expectations; experiences Bryce pinpointed in her interview with John Brown in 2002[12]:

> My remembered experience was of Thatcherism, the Hunger Strikes, memorials, protests and funerals. A lot of it was about remembering and grieving, some of it was about seeking change. I'll never forget the billboard[13] clocking up the days of hunger strikes, the black armbands, the collective anger.

Poems such as '1981' register this 'collective anger' with imagination and vigour: 'Say it with stones, say it with fire'[14] Looking back, though, in 2014, Bryce captures the imaginative power of her girlhood in Derry[15]:

> [T]he house is central to my poetic world, in its mirrors and in both of its mirrored incarnations, number 17 and number 4. And the terraced street is a concertinaed expansion of the house, a sort of cliff of rooms in and out of which many children flit like swifts. The street overlooks the valley of the town, which rises again beyond the Rossville flats to meet the crown of medieval walls. The writing is on the walls, of course, the slogans of the day in white emulsion. The house stands in its historical moment, in a particular war, where *trouble* is the norm.

12 Brown, 313.
13 As the Troubles gathered their grim harvest the present writer recalls an earlier billboard displaying the 'Scoreboard of Shame: Witness for peace' (1969–1973), established by Rev Joe Parker whose son had been gruesomely destroyed by an IRA bombing in Belfast. Crosses marked the increasing number of deaths and of those hurt in bombings. Shocking to realise that this was what was happening daily on the streets of Northern towns and villages but by such public commemorations was civic life negotiated within a tragically divided society.
14 Bryce, '1981', *Selected Poems*, 25. Other poems which concern the 'impact' of the Troubles, either directly or tangentially, include 'Last Night's Fires', 'The Analyst Couch', 'Device', 'The Brits', 'Don't Speak to the Brits …' and the shape-changing 'Helicopters'.
15 Bryce 'Omphalos', 71.

'Trouble', that is, which had an awful impact on everyone's immediate life, leading to heated squabbles amongst family and friends, complaints, yearnings and fears, so often the background to the everyday as in the father's comment in 'Satellite': '*There's nothing left/In this doom town for us;/*my mother stood her ground.'[16] In such a pressurised environment it is hardly a surprise that the counter-influences of religion remain a telling influence on Bryce's poetry[17]:

> The prayers are stamped forever into my mind, 'To Thee do we cry, poor banished children of Eve, to thee do we send out sighs, mourning and weeping in this vale of tears …', my first awareness of poetry, its rhythms and its power. The 'Desiderata' hung by the front door, its advice to 'Go placidly amid the house and haste' proving more useful on the way in than out. Hymns, also, and traditional songs.

And how this sense of another parallel world would eventually embrace all forms of communal life as the Troubles entered in the 1980s into a widespread and all-enfolding reality[18]:

> I lived and learned the strange mix of the religious, the historical and political, and the day to day. Easter is a good example of this mix, preceded by the dark penitence of Lent, then a celebration of the risen Christ, the pagan ritual of Easter eggs, and a march to commemorate the Easter Rising. The symbols of darkness and light were prevalent, the flame being passed from candle to candle in a dark cathedral at the Easter vigil blends with later memories of candlelight protest against conditions in the women's prison. It was all woven together.

In 'Derry', a central poem of Bryce's, showing powerful imaginative concentration and skill, family and community, language and landscape converge with the energetic quatrains (and an ironic nod to the opening) of Louis Mac Neice's 'iconic' poem 'Carrickfergus'[19]: 'I was born between

---

16   Bryce, 'Satellite', *Selected Poems*, 21. The 'arguing' recurs in 'Derry' as the damage and violence on the streets is internalised domestically.

17   Brown, 311.

18   Brown, 312.

19   Bryce, 'Derry', *Selected Poems*, 78–81. 'I was born in Belfast between the mountain and the gantries/ To the hooting of lost sirens and the clang of trams' 'Carrickfergus', *Louis MacNeice: Collected Poems* (London: Faber and Faber, 2007), 55.

the Creggan and the Bogside/ to the sounds of crowds and smashing glass;/ by the River Foyle with its suicides and rip tides.'

The extent and intensity of this 'strange mix of the religious, the historical and political', makes for – on reflection several years later – a powerful revelation: 'I can rarely locate the "I", a common experience in large families. Memories have a collective quality … . So the house was part of a terrace, and "I" was part of a sequence of children. Perhaps we can think of ourselves, siblings from large families, as *terraced* children, as opposed to detached or semi-detached.'[20]

'Derry' echoes the Derry of Seamus Deane's novel *Reading in the Dark* [21] so it is hardly a surprise that Bryce namechecks both in interviews and self-reflections. 'Deane's novel' she remarks to Brown, 'affected me on a level beyond the beauty of the language and its compositional grace. His realization of the place and people triggered my own memories of those streets and the stories from my mother's youth, and recognition of the layers of silences and mysteries.'[22] And again, later in 'Omphalos' she returns to the Derry Deane's novel evokes with such emotional depth and resonance[23]:

> The area, as it might have looked in my mother's heyday, was beautifully drawn by Seamus Deane in his novel *Reading in the Dark*. His characters inhabit a maze of rained-on terraces, rife with political intrigue. Where Deane's novel ends, my life begins, with the advent of the seventies.

These memories of home become all the more potent as Bryce recounts her move away from Derry in 1988[24]:

---

20 Bryce, 69.
21 Seamus Deane, *Reading in the Dark* (London: Vintage, 1996). For a further discussion of Seamus Deane as poet and novelist see Gerald Dawe, *The Wrong Country: Essays on Modern Irish Writing* (Newbridge: Irish Academic Press, 2018), 87–102.
22 Brown, 314.
23 Bryce, 70.
24 Brown, 320.

I think living elsewhere has shaped my consciousness and changed my co-ordinates. I was formed in Derry but continued to grow away from there, and I think the process of really becoming myself took place after leaving Derry. The Derry that comes into poems is definitely of the past, of memory, perceived by myself of that time. That said, I consider Derry home and probably always will. If I had stayed, I might be a very different writer, or exactly the same, or not be writing at all. I'll never know.

The notion of leaving home and returning forms a strong thematic rhythm in Northern Irish writing with poets such as John Montague, Padraic Fiacc, Seamus Heaney and Derek Mahon. Their poetry is often based upon journeys home in real and imagined time. As Bryce had it in the conclusion of 'Derry'[25] 'I watched that place grow small'. But time and distance are not quite as critical as Bryce reflected in her closing remarks to John Brown in that 2002 interview[26]: 'I come hurtling into Derry as often as I can – Ryan Air speciality… Derry has changed a lot since I left in 1988, for the better. Every visit home seemed to reveal new buildings and the city has healed a lot, visibly and psychologically, since I lived there. There's a good atmosphere there, and for me it still feels like a safe place.' Precious wonder then that poems are often set 'in transit', in spaces prior to flight, or post-return, in airplanes awaiting lift-off, in the pauses in Belfast before the home-run, or figuratively in the 'time-lapse footage'[27] of life itself, as living reaches final stages; a glimpse here or there; the ever fleeting 'now'.

The achievement of Bryce's collection *The M Pages* is partly based on how the poet has imagined the loss that death brings in its wake. It is as if the past is always here but evasively so and the poetic act captures what has gone as in the tender poem 'Hire Car', about her mother's moving towards end of life.[28]

In one of the finest elegies of recent years 'The M Pages' sequence, Bryce imagines loss with a dramatic conversation between poems which recount the death of a beloved sister and the way grief is 'managed', eye to eye, with a hint of Plath's statement-led imagery.[29]

25   Bryce, 'Derry', *Selected Poems*, 81.
26   Brown, 321.
27   Bryce, 'Fungi', *The M Pages*, 20.
28   Bryce, 'Hire Car', *The M Pages*, 18.
29   Bryce, '13', *The M Pages*, 41.

Similarly, Bryce's imaginative return to the family house is reproduced with the lure of a film director. 'My recent poems' she writes, 'seem to want to examine that place, and time, more closely. The results are only glimpses, seen through doorways, sometimes held in mirrors. The mirror in our hallway was consulted by everyone leaving or entering by the front door – checking faces, fixing hair. Now, in the hall mirror, I can see nine children looking out. I'm stealing this image from a Mary Poppins story, where a small boy asks her to tell him what he looks like. "Look in the mirror", she says, surprised. "But there are so many faces", he replies, "I don't know which is mine!"'[30]

Almost two decades later when, in an interview with Adam Wyeth in 2018[31] Bryce responds to his question about the UK Brexit referendum's result and asks 'has it ignited anything in' her poetry:

> It's clarified my desire to move back to Ireland. I value Irish literary culture more and more, as a kind of deceitful populism becomes the norm in the UK … Poets have always worked away quietly on the margins, and I like that. You get little response. It takes resilience to keep going, and a faith in the process. Geographically, I've always felt homeless in my adult life …. I travel a lot these days, which I love, including to Ireland often. I feel oddly at home in transit.

The perennial theme of home and its pull both emotional and imaginative is neatly caught in Bryce's response to a further telling question (from Conor O'Callaghan)when in relation to the final poem in *The Full Indian Rope Trick* '+'[32] he notes that the poem 'admits "we …. haven't taken off at all"' and lands right back into 'Irish rain' and asks "Does every poet have material that is inescapable" ':

> I've travelled around a lot since I left Ireland at 18, and I've lived in a number of cities. There's been a price to pay for all of that moving around, but there's also been a lot to gain, from the places and people. Emigration was and is a key experience in my life …. Not a single experience but a continuous one. The idea of home grows ever more elusive.

30 Bryce, 71.
31 Adam Wyeth, "Colette Bryce", *The Manchester Review: Non-Fiction* (Issue 23, 2020) online: www.themanchesterreview.co.uk
32 Bryce, '+', *Selected Poems,* 44.

In many ways this final statement summarises not just the experiences of Bryce's more liberated generation – when air travel became second nature and mobility the default position for hundreds and thousands of younger Irish women and men. But also, the 'idea of home' itself becomes so much less a 'given', inherited and conditioned by specific experiences, but rather something re-created and imagined; a freer, more open sense of the past that follows a deeper and more complex understanding of how and why one's own experiences, lived away from family and home, are mirrored in (or challenged by) the lives of others outside the community of one's upbringing.

The gloriously titled poem 'The theatrical death of my maternal grandmother as revealed in a 1960s glitter globe' plays with the distinctly Derry woman's voice, breaking through the much-vaunted and discussed Northern way of non-saying.[33] The poem's conversation about 'the premiere/ 'on Broadway!' of/ *Philadelphia, Here I Come!*'[34] reveals with pride, irony and liveliness, a powerful centre to unfolding histories and about 'getting on', as the poem rhetorically has it.

Bryce's poetry is an important critical yet intimate part of such a welcome and liberating maturation. Her point on 'form', for instance, is well stated, if outside the scope of the current essay's concerns, along with several other important attributes and themes in her writing I haven't touched on here: 'I don't consider any poem to be without form. Successful poems adhere to inner music, inner forms. Formally, I write for the ear more than for the eye. Some is learned, some is instinct.'[35] With such a sophisticated vernacular sound system, its lithe but unpretentious playfulness, and its ability to conjure with the rights and wrongs of how we see things, matched by an unerring sense of literary precedent, Colette Bryce is the most emotionally adept and challenging poet of her generation – an unmistakable voice who is extending on her own ground the celebrated achievements of Seamus Heaney and Seamus Deane, the two other poets most publicly identified with the north-west of Ireland.

---

33 Bryce, 'The theatrical death of my maternal grandmother as revealed in a 1960s glitter globe', *Selected Poems*, 86. The reference is to Brian Friel's ground-breaking play first performed in 1964.

34 Brown, 317.

35 'The famous// Northern reticence, the tight gag of place/And times' as Seamus Heaney has it in his poem 'Whatever You Say Say Nothing', *North* (London: Faber and Faber, 1975), 59.

CHAPTER 7

Without a City Wall: Gail McConnell

There is a green hill far away,
without a city wall,
where the dear Lord was crucified,
who died to save us all.[1]

Two things strike me when I think about the history of Irish poetry in the twentieth century. Firstly, the way in which the great figures of Irish protestant hymn-writing such as C. F. Alexander have been in some way elided from the canon. Bearing in mind just how popular and integrated such hymns from the Protestant traditions are in the world it seems strange that little has been done in more recent years to integrate this extensive global writing into the wider reaches of Irish literary history. The second 'issue' is also a matter of elision. Irish poetry is widely considered to be non-experimental when in fact this is quite clearly not the case. Undoubtedly the best-known and critically recognised poets from Ireland, writing in English, fit formally into the English poetic mainstream – such as those discussed earlier in these pages. So, it might be timely to close this sequence of readings by looking briefly at a poet whose cultural background and literary and intellectual range merge – at least in part – these absences in poems of extraordinary poignancy, emotional depth and (crucially) playfulness.

---

1   Cecil Frances Alexander 'There is a Green Hill Far away', *Trinity Psalter Hymnal*, #347.

   Cecil Frances Humphries b. Redcross, County Wicklow, Ireland, 1818; Londonderry, Ireland, 1895. In 1850 she married Rev. William Alexander, who later became the Anglican primate of Ireland. Alexander was strongly influenced by the Oxford Movement and by John Keble's Christian Year. Her first book of poetry, *Verses for Seasons*, was a 'Christian Year' for children. She wrote hymns based on the Apostles' Creed, baptism, the Lord's Supper and the Ten Commandments.

Gail McConnell was born in Belfast in 1980. Her educational achievements are substantial as are her current academic responsibilities as a senior
lecturer in English at Queen's University Belfast.[2] She has published an
important and challenging study *Northern Irish Poetry and Theology*[3] but
it is to her poetry that I am turning in what follows, in particular the long
poem 'Type Face',[4] and, most recently, and most pertinently to my theme,
The Sun is Open,[5] one of the most form-changing, spirited and exhilarating
books of poetry (or maybe that should be book-length poems) by an Irish
poet which I have read in quite some time.

The centripetal moment, which draws into coherence what I have to say
about this fascinatingly different material, is the tragic (tragic beyond words,
I was going to say) death of the poet's young father, William McConnell,
murdered by an IRA 'unit' in March 1984. This is how the magisterial *Lost
Lives* recounts the shocking killing[6]:

March 6, 1984

William McConnell, East Belfast

Prison officer, Protestant, 35, married, 1 Child

An assistant governor at the Maze[7] where he was in charge of security, he was shot in
the driveway of his home at Hawthornden Drive off Belmont Road. He was shot in

2   See: <https://pure.qub.ac.uk/en/persons/gail-mcconnell>.
3   Gail McConnell, *Northern Irish Poetry and Theology* (Basingstoke: Palgrave
     Macmillan, 2014).
4   McConnell, 'Type Face', *Blackbox Manifold* (Issue 17, 2016).
5   McConnell has also published two pamphlets – *Fourteen* (London: Green Bottle
     Press, 2018) and *Fothermather* (London: Ink Sweat and Tears Press, 2019). *The Sun
     is Open* (London: Penned *in the Margins*, 2021).
6   David McKittrick, Seamus Kelters, Brian Feeney and Chris Thornton (eds), *Lost
     Lives: The Stories of the Men, Women and Children Who Died as a Result of the
     Northern Ireland Troubles* (Edinburgh and London: Mainstream Publishing,
     2001), 979.
7   The Maze, Her Majesty's Prison Maze was previously Long Kesh Detention Centre
     but also known as The Maze (or H-Block)was a prison in Northern Ireland that
     housed paramilitary prisoners during the Northern Irish Troubles from 1971
     to 2000.

front of his wife and three-year-old daughter as he checked the underside of his car for booby-traps. He left a letter in which he referred to the possibility of his death.

The context of the attack, post Hunger Strikes of 1981 and the mass jail-break of republican prisoners in 1983, is particularly grim as the note to the entries for 1984 in *Lost Lives* make plain: 'Thirty-eight of the 72 dead were civilians, nine were RUC officers, nine were regular soldiers and ten were UDR members. Twelve republicans and one loyalist also died. Republicans were responsible for 51 of the deaths, loyalists for 10 and the security forces for 11.'[8] The cruel matrix of such suffering is well beyond the scope of this chapter but the echo is stark when one revisits the loss of life which is such a key dramatic focus in O'Casey's Dublin plays (see above) while asking the moral questions about the political and ideological reasons behind such damage throughout spasmatic periods of modern Irish history.

Fast forward and change location from Dublin to Belfast and new and deeply troubling questions arise when the civic toll of all this human suffering is weighed alongside the conditions out of which the violence was seeded. In this particular 'case' though the personal and the political, the familial and the cultural are meshed into a stunningly real yet imaginative revisioning of 'what happened'.

Thirty years after the murder, the loss is alluded to in the dedication to Gail McConnell's study of poetry and theology in Northern Ireland: 'For my father, William McConnell whose absent presence creates the questions'[9]; questions which 'Type Face' revisits with a provocatively destabilising tone and élan based upon the Historical Enquiries Team Report.[10] This is the opening to the seven-part poem of over 300 lines of generally rhyming couplets[11]:

The thing I notice noticing's the font

8   McKittrick et al., *Lost Lives*, 973.
9   McConnell, *Northern Irish Poetry and Theology*, verso.
10   Historical Enquiries Team Reports: The Historical Enquiries Team was set up in 2005 to investigate thousands of unsolved murders committed during the Troubles, between mostly 1968 and 1998. The unit was disbanded in September 2014.
11   McConnell, '*Type Face*: 1'

in the Historical Enquiries Team Report.
It's Comic Sans. Comic Sans!

The font is 'of parish news and Christmas fares' and from this point the poem takes off into an extraordinary journey into the way grief, recollection, the past and present, living and death form around the wound of loss while the 'official' rendering of a crime[12] is shaped and delivered in such a tactless, thoughtless format, beggars belief.

'Typeface' is a kind of anti-war war poem because it reveals both the cruelty of war (civil war), the aftermath of memory and commemoration through raising the question of how survivors continue with their lives, living with loss and endeavouring to understand the reasons why, the contexts of violence and the responsibilities for what happened during the brutal northern conflict. But at the core of 'Typeface' there is another story, or perspective based upon the cultural and emotional place of home – the reality of a home, that is, traumatised by violence – and the upbringing the poet experienced within Northern Protestantism[13]:

> I'm struck by nothing
> once again 'My hope is Built on Nothing
> Less …' – first their wedding, then his funeral.
> This wish for solid ground.

Edward Mote's hymn[14] 'gives voice to so much isolation' the poet remarks, 'I grew up with these verses, on the blue /itchy carpet tiles (they'd pulled out all the pews)/ of a tiny Baptist church'. And the sampling begins:

---

12 Thomas Kinsella's *Butcher's Dozen: A Lesson for the Octave of Widgery* (1972) was written in response to a British judicial review, The Widgery Report, long discredited as a 'whitewash' of the unlawful killing of thirteen unarmed citizens on 30 January 1972 by paratroopers of the First Battalion Parachute Regiment in Derry/ Londonderry. Both poems provide an unsettling comparison between the convergence of personal loss, ideological justification and political connivance of states in civic crisis.

13 McConnell, '*Type Face*: VI'

14 Mote, 'My Hope is Built on Nothing Less' also includes the lines; 'His oath, his covenant and blood/, Support me in the sinking flood/, when all around my soul

> *There is a green hill*
> *Far away, without a city wall.*
> *When we've been there ten thousand years; Abide*
> *With me; fast falls the eventide.*

The language, imagery and vision of Protestantism is a subject all to itself, but the influence of this culture is markedly present in McConnell's poetry at various different levels: as the backdrop to her recalled childhood, as a semantic principle of representation and as the provider of metaphor and (quite literarily) music: 'Imprint, O Lord, thy word'[15]

> He touches his face
> his thumb
>
>   the spirals turning inward
>   oil and smoke, a siren somewhere, eyelids start
>   to close
>   lips met
>   and part
>   in the – O -- O – O --
> of prayer

Will Loxley in 'Where are the War Poets?', the concluding chapter to his Second World War study, *Writing in the Dark*[16] quotes the American poet and anthologist Oscar Williams asking the question whether 'most people do not have the courage to face honestly the facts of others' intense suffering?' Williams goes on to state: 'It is easier to have the attention diverted, conscience soothed and the guilt of responsibility converted into

---

gives way/He then is all my hope and stay'. Edward Mote (Baptist pastor and hymn writer, 1797–1874). <https://www.Hymnologyarchive.com/solid-rock>.

15 McConnell, 'Imprint, O Lord, thy word', *Fourteen*, 24. In an email the poet provides the following context: 'Imprint, O Lord, thy word' has in mind the Ballymurphy massacre and in particular the story of Father Hugh Mullan, who went to the aid of his neighbour and was shot in the back.' (email: 2 November 2021). Both innocent victims, Father Hugh Mullan (38) and Francis Quinn (19) were shot dead by soldiers of B Company 2 Parachute Regiment in an area of open ground in Springfield Park, Belfast, 9 August 1971.

16 Will Loxley, *Writing in the Dark: Bloomsbury, the Blitz and Horizon Magazine* (London: Weidenfeld & Nicolson, 2021), 344.

a conviction that the suffering is justified since it is in a noble cause.'[17]
The manner in which McConnell has transformed the legacy of loss – an
'intense suffering' handed down through almost four decades of absence
and the presence of this 'void', the repeated shock of the moment of the
killing, the 'scene' – makes this aspect of her writing hugely relevant to
an audience which may well prefer not to 'face honestly' what happened
in real time to real people. That bridge into reality, rather than the ideological or culture wars of particular political positions, is what poetry provides; particularly poetry of the first rank. As Adam Piette stated in his
review of *The Sun is Open*: 'What the poems might be said to be doing is
lifting the blanking of trauma out of the silences at the back of news and
into the print space of the poem we are reading.'[18] He asserts:

> [*The Sun is Open*] is a murder book and it is not; for its pressing into type of the
> thing of trauma is a dislodging of the subject out of the room of powerful elegy into
> edge-space aslant; and its sequence is something of a revelation, stitching together
> text, archive, memory with found material and obstinate self-questioning that makes
> this one of the most startling elegies in print.

I agree whole-heartedly. There is nothing sentimental, exploitative or
'knowing' in Gail McConnell's re-imagining of what happened because
her imagination is utterly grounded in language and its forms on a page;
the sheer physicality of words written, miswritten, misheard; misused
and the shape of language too – traversing the lawn of a page, busted-
up, broken into smithereens or rebuilt visually: these are all parts of
McConnell's speech patterns as we look and see what she makes language
'do'[19]:

> I had a sound for you by it I
> called you daaaaaaaaaa deee
> you had one for me the name you

17   *The War Poets: An Anthology of the war poets of the 20th century*, edited by Oscar
      Williams (New York: The John Jay Company, 1945), 5.
18   Adam Piette 'Review: Anna Mendelssohn and Gail McConnell', *blackbox manifold*
      (Issue 26, Summer 2021), online.
19   Mc Connell, *The Sun is Open*, 42.

gave me between one and two
syllables geeeaaal you called me
your twice-voiced dawwww ter

There are some Irish parallels though French poets such as Apollinaire
come to mind. I am thinking here of less well-known poets such as Brian
Coffey (in his *Death of Hektor*,[20] for instance) or the Belfast poet, Padraic
Fiacc[21] who took poetic form into a space not so dissimilar from McConnell
but without her restraint and intellectual control. For the latter the comparison is with fellow Belfast poet Derek Mahon, one of the three poets
McConnell focusses upon in her study of Northern Irish poetry.

In the concluding chapter to this book 'The only way out of "the
tongue-tied profanity": Calvinism, rupture and revision in the poetry
of Derek Mahon' she writes persuasively on Mahon. He is 'a Protestant
poet, but a Protestantism that insists on the metaphysical rupture between
subject and object, and between the would-be subject and the would-be
Protestant community or would-be Protestant ideology, and a poetry that
is never perfected'.[22]

She continues by connecting and interpreting, the significance of
Mahon's poetry, in particular 'Matthew 29–30' to that which 'illuminates
Northern Irish religious and political culture' – 'The violence it signals
is not only personal but also political. The widespread critical failure to
adequately acknowledge the violent impetus of Mahon's textual practice
and the context in which it takes shape reveals vital assumptions underpin-
ning Northern Irish literary criticism.'[23] With the full force of belief and
explication behind her, McConnell's conclusion sounds almost biblical in
itself: 'The poet speaks for no one, including himself, and he destroys even

20 Brian Coffey, *Poems and Versions 1925–1990* (Dublin: Dedalus Press, 1991). See also
    Other Edens: The Life and Work of Brian Coffey, edited by Benjamin Keatinge and
    Aengus Woods (Dublin: Irish Academic Press, 2010).

21 Padraic Fiacc, *Ruined Pages: New Selected Poems*, edited by Gerald Dawe and
    Aodan MacPoilin (Derry: Lagan Press, 2012). See also *My Twentieth Century Night
    Life: A Padraic Fiacc Miscellany,* ed. Patrick Ramsey (Belfast: Lagan Press, 1996).
    Fiacc often spoke of his sense of his poetry as reproducing 'smithereens'.

22 Mc Connell, 219.

23 Mc Connell, 234.

an imagined community of readers; the liberal-humanist conscience, vexed to nightmare, becomes masochistic; the aesthetic offers neither sanctuary nor escape – it is tortured and torturous, doing violence to its textual body and to its reader.'[24]

It is possible to turn these phrases back towards McConnell's poetry too. In *The Sun is Open* the cultural and religious web out of which the sequence of prose-poems emerge is heavily inflected with both Protestantism and a literature of disruption: Genesis, Jonah, Ruth, Judges, *The Book of Common Prayer*, connect with contemporary archival references – to local newspapers *The Belfast Telegraph* and *The News Letter*, the music of Ralph Mc Tell, Lennon and McCartney, her father's diaries of 1967–1968, family witness statements of his murder, Hansard official reports, IRA statements on the killing and its 'justification' as well as learnings from Shakespeare (*Othello* and *The Tempest*), Keats, Cowper and Foucault.

This might all sound breathlessly jangled but it actually fits into place under the abiding exhortation of Protestant self-scrutiny (what used to be called 'shriving') but re-energised and made lively and convincingly present because the composition of the poem(s), in Ciaran Carson's words 'deal with issues of the utmost gravity – matters of life and death – nevertheless display a rueful lightness of touch'.[25] Qualities long held to characterise the deft and light-filled landscapes of Mahon's poetry. If Mahon's 'Matthew V. 29–30' provides a key text for McConnell's study of poetic theologies it might well be that there is a closer parallel to be found in 'A Refusal to Mourn', another poem from the same Mahon collection, *The Snow Party*.[26]

Dedicated to fellow northern writer Maurice Leitch, Mahon describes his relative 'the old man' who, in 'a small farmhouse/at the edge of a new estate', lives alone after decades of a working life in the (Belfast) shipyards:

24   McConnell, ibid.
25   Ciaran Carson endorsement quoted on the fly-leaf of *The Sun is Open*.
26   Derek Mahon, 'A Refusal to Mourn', *The Snow Party* (London: Oxford University Press, 1975), 34. Unlike the fate of 'Matthew V.29–30', deleted from the Mahon canon of various selected and collected editions, 'A Refusal to Mourn' has been retained.

But the secret bred in the bone
on the dawn strand survives
in other times and lives,
persisting for the unborn
like a claw-print in concrete
after the bird has flown.

The apocalyptic ending, like the existential gaze of the old man, brings such pristine closure to Mahon's poem that it seems to release the reader into a much more intense and intimate feeling for life itself. This is something Gail McConnell shares in her own very distinctive achievement as poet (and, it should be stressed, in thematic areas and forms not touched upon here) and as an original thinker.

Afterword: Engaging Poems

William Carlos Williams's 'Asphodel, That Greeny Flower', an epic-like poem divided into three sections or 'books' which concludes with a 'Coda', has always fascinated me. It is a deeply felt love poem, addressed to Flossie, Carlos Williams's wife of over forty years. But it is also a poem that meditates upon the political events of his time of writing – the early 1950s. Indeed, the poem is in part a defining expression of the anxieties of that time in North America. And 'Asphodel' concerns the poet's art of memory, of how poetry is itself a form of commemoration, an embodiment of the past and of how that which is important and necessary is retained by poetry. It is, too, a poetic confession, as Williams alludes to his indiscretions and failures as a husband and as a father.

The poem ranges with wonderfully intimate ease across many cultures, epochs and art form to visit other countries and places from Switzerland and Spain, to Venice and south-west France while simultaneously rooting itself in the specific local and familiar surroundings of the poet's home and family life in Rutherford, New Jersey and along the seascapes of the east coast of his childhood and maturity: 'There are the starfish' he recalls, 'stiffened by the sun/and other sea wrack/and weeds. We know that/along with the rest of it/ for we were born by the sea, / knew its rose hedges/to the very water's edge.'[1] What he calls elsewhere in the poem 'the fields/ which we knew/as children.'[2]

The most important and obvious feature of the poem is its *spoken-ness*. 'Asphodel, That Greeny Flower' has all the energy, pace and hesitations of a man talking and on the understanding he is addressing an 'other' – his beloved wife. Beyond that initiating monologue, we too are his auditors,

---

1   William Carlos Williams, *Journey to Love* (New York: Random House, 1955), 47–48. All quotations from 'Asphodel, That Greeny Flower' are taken from this edition.
2   Carlos Williams, 'Asphodel', 79.

listening in on the (Shakespearean-like) soliloquy as if we were listening and watching the dramatic speech of a suburban King Lear.

The conscientious acting out of this life story is occasioned in 'Asphodel' by Carlos Williams's failing health and surrounding causes, as Paul Mariani makes clear in his biography of the poet: 'Williams began [*Asphodel*] thinking that he was beginning a fifth book of *Paterson*' but the poem which 'was to occupy him for the better part of two years' [1953–55] is marked by 'the period of his most severe incapacitation and mental depression'.[3]

Simply put, Carlos Williams was 70 years old in 1953. He has already suffered a heart attack and the previous year, the first of a series of strokes that would ultimately led to his death, ten years later, in 1963. The stroke has, however, coincided with an extraordinary grim time in American social and cultural life, which had seen Senator Joe McCarthy whip up a frenzy over communist infiltration in the media, university and political institutions.

When his name was associated with the Library of Congress Consultant, Carlos Williams came under suspicion as a one-time communist sympathiser. The Federal Employees Loyalty Programme was evoked and he was to be investigated by the FBI before the offer of the position could be formally made. The legal situation regarding the appointment deteriorated into a farce which humiliated the doctor-poet. As a result of the stroke and his temporary incapacity to write (or read), Williams suffered an intense bout of depression and was hospitalised in Hillside Hospital, Floral Park, Queens where he remained for eight weeks – 'a living hell' he called it,[4] though he did respect the time he spent there, meeting with others in a like situation as himself.

The only permitted contact with the outside world was via letters to Flossie. Disorientated, with the use of only his left hand, those eight months between his first stroke and the release from hospital in 1953 are the summoning context out of which 'Asphodel' was to emerge. Most crucially, it was also the period in which he confessed in writing those letters

---

3   Paul Mariani, *William Carlos Williams: A New World Naked* (New York: W. W. Norton, 1981), 670.
4   Mariani, *William Carlos Williams*, 660.

to his wife his past failings as she in turn was to guide him back to health, reading to him from an extensive array of poetry and related work. As his recovery took hold, 'Asphodel' was to become Williams's testament to that time but also, retrospectively, to their lives together as man and wife. The poem was finally published in 1955 in *Journey to Love*, as the culmination of a collection of fifteen additional poems all of which are characterised by 'the step-down line of variable measure' through which Williams sought to capture the idiomatic syntax of American English and the sound of a man talking directly of what he sees and feels and imagines.

If 'Asphodel' originates in what his biographer describes as 'a heavy incidence of personal memories'[5] some of which Williams had recorded in his prose writings, such as his *Autobiography* (1951) and later on in *I Wanted to Write a Poem* (1958), there are various cross-currents weaving in and out of the text in what Mariani refers to as 'a design of mathematical purity … a calculus of persuasions.'[6] It would not be feasible to analyse here each and every one of these elements but rather take a broader view and portray the kind of mosaic that 'Asphodel' adds up to, before concluding with reference to the concluding lines of Book 1.

At the heart of 'Asphodel' there is the infusing image of the flower itself, and its symbolic power as both an 'ordinary' flower but also, in Greek mythology, the flowers of Hell. This Homeric trope sits alongside the suburban local settings of the poem and varies the focus from myth to the domestic and back again with uncomplicated transitions. Other flowers are called to our mind but it is the asphodel that almost physically assumes pre-eminence as the lines move up and down the page as tender yet persistent offshoots from an adaptive textual stem, some short, some long, tended by the act of poetic attention in parallel to Flossie's actual gathering care:

> It is winter
>   and there
>   waiting for you to care for them
> are your plants.
>   Poor things! you say

5   Mariani, 671.
6   Mariani, 670.

>   as you compassionately
>   pour at their roots
>   the reviving water.[7]

The image of Flossie and the image of the flowers merge into a life-affirming epiphany of love within the boundaries of a long-standing marriage. That it survives the blasts of truth-telling and the realities of forgiveness is however only part of the emotional story the poem dramatises. For the light of Carlos Williams's life is overshadowed by darker forces such as the nuclear holocaust that the Bomb represented in people's mind during the fifties' Cold War. The destructiveness of societies – be that in the US, with the execution by electric chair of Julius and Ethel Rosenberg in June 1953 on charges of spying for the Soviet Union, or in Argentina with the Peronist burning down of the Jockey Club Buenos Aires, along with its priceless artworks and library, or going back in time to the Salem Witch Trials of seventeenth-century New England – these examples show what the forces of good must withstand in order to survive the imminence of death and death-dealing. But the powerful simplicities of art will always be there – the nuptial songs of Spenser, Chaucer, John Donne; the grandeur of the physical landscapes such as Jungfrau in Switzerland, Granada in Spain; the visual miracles of cave paintings in south-western France to Carlos Williams and Flossie's painter-friend, Charles Demuth – a watercolourist whose frail health led to his early death in 1935 – and the human presence of the statue of the 15th soldier, Colleoni in Venice, as well as the numerous name checks of artists and writers from Homer to Herman Melville, Cezanne, Darwin and Columbus to Tolstoy … .The balance of 'Asphodel' is tilted away from what the poet called 'the world's niggardliness' towards 'fortitude' and the light of the imagination.

'Asphodel, that greeny flower' is full of ordinary people too – those close to the poet, like his father, and his father's ghostly reappearance in the subway; his friends – artists of one kind or another – and the pale shimmering eroticism of women throughout his life, resolve into the enduring vision of Flossie, on their wedding day, almost half a century previously:

---

7   Carlos Williams, *Journey to Love*, 76.

> I thought the world
> stood still.
>   At the altar
>   so intent was I
> before my vows,
>   so moved by your presence
>   a girl so pale [8]

The sentiment can be degraded by reading sentimentality into the text but that would be a pity and a miscuing of the intentness of Carlos Williams's design. Borne of such fascinating multi-cultural roots and resources, at a time of great international conflict and diplomatic crises that shaped his daily professional life as a full-time doctor and pediatrician, this magnificent poem of Carlos Williams carries within it all the stresses and strains of an actual adult relationship between two people whose love for each other and the world they know (and in part created) had reached through the darkness towards a kind of definitive light of self-understanding. The pleasure and sensual music of William Carlos Williams's lines are matched by the musculature of that reasoning and arguing with himself and the sheer joy in witnessing the world for its own sake. What more can a poet be asked for? How else should a poem, or novel, or play engage us? Isn't this what literature is really about, when all is said and done?

8   Carlos Williams, 86.

Bibliography

Atik, Anne, *How It Was: A Memoir of Samuel Beckett* (London: Thames and Hudson, 2001).

Bair, Deirdre, *Samuel Beckett: A Biography* (London: Picador, 1980).

Beckett, Samuel, *Watt* (London: Faber and Faber, 2009. Orig. Paris: Olympia Press, 1953).

——, *Disjecta: Miscellaneous Writings and a Dramatic Fragment*, edited with a foreword by Ruby Cohn (London: John Calder, 1983).

Boland, Eavan, *Object Lessons: The Life of the Woman and the Poet in Our Time* (London: Vintage 1996).

Brown, John, ed. *In the Chair: Interviews with Poets from the North of Ireland* (Cliffs of Moher: Salmon Press, 2002).

Brown, Terence, *Ireland's Literature: Selected Essays* (Dublin: Lilliput Press, 1988).

——, *The Life of W. B. Yeats* (Oxford: Blackwell Publishers, 1999).

Bryce, Colette, *The Heel of Bernadette* (London: Picador 2000).

——, *The Full Indian Rope Trick* (London: Picador, 2004).

——, *Self Portrait in the Dark* (London: Picador, 2008).

——, 'Omphalos: Returning to the troubles of a Northern Irish childhood', *Poetry* (Vol. 205. No. 1) October 2014.

——, *Selected Poems* (London: Picador, 2017).

——, *The M Pages* (London: Picador, 2020).

Coffey, Brian, *Poems and Versions 1929–1990* (Dublin: Dedalus Press, 1991).

Connolly, Peter (ed.), *Literature and the Changing Ireland* (Gerrards Cross: Colin Smythe, 1982).

Dawe, Gerald, *Of War and War's Alarms* (Cork: Cork University Press, 2015).

——, *The Wrong County: Essays on Modern Irish Writing* (Newbridge: Irish Academic Press, 2018).

Deane, Seamus, *Reading in the Dark* (London: Vintage, 1996).

Dunn, Douglas (ed.), *Two Decades of Irish Writing, A Critical Survey* (Cheadle, Cheshire: Carcanet Press, 1975).

Durcan, Paul, 'The Drumshambo Hustler: A celebration of Van Morrison', *Magill*, May 1988.

——, *A Snail in My Prime: New and Selected Poems* (London: The Harvill Press / Belfast: Blackstaff Press, 1993).

Fallon, Peter, ed., *Chosen Lights: Poets on Poems by John Montague* (Oldcastle: Gallery Press, 2009).

Farrell, James Gordon, *The Lung* (London: Corgi Books, 1967 [orig. 1965]).

Fiacc, Padraic, *Ruined Pages: New Selected Poems* (Derry: Lagan Press, 2012).

Grene, Nicholas, *The Politics of Irish Drama: Plays in Context from Boucicault to Friel* (Cambridge: Cambridge University Press, 1999).

Heaney, Seamus, *North* (London: Faber and Faber, 1975).

——, *Finders Keepers Selected Prose 1971–2001* (London: Faber and Faber, 2002).

——, *W. B. Yeats: Poet to Poet* (London: Faber and Faber, 2004).

Homer, *The Odyssey*, translated by Walter Shewring with an introduction by G. S. Kirk (Oxford/New York: Oxford University Press, 1980).

James, Joyce, *Dubliners* (London: Jonathan Cape 1934 [original pub 1914]).

Kavanagh, Patrick, *Collected Poems* (London: Allen Lane, 2004).

Kearns, Kevin C., *Dublin Tenement Life: An Oral History* (Dublin: Gill & Macmillan, 2006).

Keatinge, Benjamin and Aengus Woods (eds), *Other Edens: The Life and work of Brian Coffey* (Dublin: Irish Academic Press, 2010).

Longley, Michael, 'A Jovial Hullaballoo', *One Wide Expanse: Writing from the Ireland Chair of Poetry* (Dublin: University College Dublin Press, 2015).

Loxley, Will, *Writing in the Dark: Bloomsbury, the Blitz and Horizon Magazine* (London: Weidenfeld & Nicolson, 2021).

McCarrick, Jacqueline, 'A New Thing Breathing: The Landscape Art of Patrick Kavanagh', M. Phil in Irish Writing paper (Dublin: Trinity College Dublin, April 2004).

McConnell, Gail, *Northern Irish Poetry and Theology* (Basingstoke: Palgrave Macmillan, 2014*)*.

——, *Fourteen* (London: Green Bottle Press, 2018).

——, *Fothermother* (London: Ink Sweat and Tears Press, 2019).

——, *The Sun is Open* (London: Penned *in the margins*, 2021).

McKittrick, David, Seamus Kelters, Brian Feeney and Chris Thornton (eds), *Lost Lives: The Stories of the Men, Women and Children Who Died as a Result of the Northern Ireland Troubles* (Edinburgh and London: Mainstream Publishing, 2001).

MacNeice, Louis, *The Poetry of W B Yeats* (London: Faber and Faber, 1941).

——, *Collected Poems* (London: Faber and Faber, 2007).

Mahon, Derek, *New Collected Poems* (Oldcastle: Gallery Press, 2011).

——, *Selected Prose* (Oldcastle: The Gallery Press, 2012).

Mariani, Paul, *William Carlos Williams: A New World Naked* (New York: W. W. Norton, 1981).

Maxwell, Desmond Ernest Stewart, *Modern Irish Drama* (Cambridge: Cambridge University Press, 1984).

Montague, John, *The Figure in the Cave and Other Essays* (Dublin: Lilliput Press, 1989).

——, *New Collected Poems* (Oldcastle: Gallery Press, 2012).

Morash, Christopher, *A History of Irish Theatre, 1601–2000* (Cambridge: Cambridge University Press, 2002).

Muldoon, Paul, *Meeting the British* (London: Faber and Faber, 1987).

Murphy, Richard, *The Kick: A Life among Writers* (London: Granta, 2003).

O'Brien, Joseph Valentine, *"Dear Dirty Dublin": A City in Distress, 1899–1916* (California: University of California Press, 1992).

O'Callaghan, Conor, ed., *The Wake Forest Series of Irish Poetry* (Winston-Salem: Wake Forest, 2013).

O'Casey, Sean, *Three Dublin Plays*, introduced by Christopher Murray (London: Faber and Faber, 1998).

Prunty, Jacinta, 'From City Slums to City Sprawl: Dublin from 1890 to the Present', *Irish Cities*, edited by Howard Clarke (Cork: Mercier Press, 1995).

Seferis, George, *Collected Poems*, translated, edited, and introduced by Edmund Keeley and Philip Sherrard (London: Anvil Press, 1982).

Thomas, Kinsella, *Collected Poems, 1956–1994* (Manchester: Carcanet Press, 1996).

Thompson, William Irwin, *The Imagination of an Insurrection: Dublin Easter 1916* (New York: Oxford University Press, 1967).

Yeats, William Butler, 'Four Years: 1887–1891', *Autobiographies* (London: Macmillan, 1980 [1955]).

——, *Letters on Poetry from W. B. Yeats to Dorothy Wellesley* (London: Oxford University Press, 1964).

——, *W. B. Yeats The Poems*, edited by Daniel Albright (London: J. M. Dent & Sons, 1990).

——, *The Collected Works of W. B. Yeats: Vol II The Plays*, edited by David R. Clark and Rosalind E. Clark (Basingstoke: Palgrave, 2001).

Williams, Oscar, *The War Poets: An anthology of the war poets of the 20th century* (New York: The John Jay Company, 1945).

Williams, William Carlos, *Journey to Love* (New York: Random House, 1955).

Wyeth, Adam, 'Colette Bryce', *The Manchester Review: Non-Fiction* (Issue 23, 2018).

Reimagining Ireland

Series Editor: Dr Eamon Maher, Technological University Dublin

The concepts of Ireland and 'Irishness' are in constant flux in the wake of an ever-increasing reappraisal of the notion of cultural and national specificity in a world assailed from all angles by the forces of globalisation and uniformity. Reimagining Ireland interrogates Ireland's past and present and suggests possibilities for the future by looking at Ireland's literature, culture and history and subjecting them to the most up-to-date critical appraisals associated with sociology, literary theory, historiography, political science and theology.

Some of the pertinent issues include, but are not confined to, Irish writing in English and Irish, Nationalism, Unionism, the Northern 'Troubles', the Peace Process, economic development in Ireland, the impact and decline of the Celtic Tiger, Irish spirituality, the rise and fall of organised religion, the visual arts, popular cultures, sport, Irish music and dance, emigration and the Irish diaspora, immigration and multiculturalism, marginalisation, globalisation, modernity/postmodernity and postcolonialism. The series publishes monographs, comparative studies, interdisciplinary projects, conference proceedings and edited books. Proposals should be sent either to Dr Eamon Maher at eamon.maher@ittdublin.ie or to ireland@peterlang.com.

Vol. 1   Eugene O'Brien: 'Kicking Bishop Brennan up the Arse': Negotiating Texts and Contexts in Contemporary Irish Studies
ISBN 978-3-03911-539-6. 219 pages. 2009.

Vol. 2   James P.Byrne, Padraig Kirwan and Michael O'Sullivan (eds): Affecting Irishness: Negotiating Cultural Identity Within and Beyond the Nation
ISBN 978-3-03911-830-4. 334 pages. 2009.

Vol. 3   Irene Lucchitti: The Islandman: The Hidden Life of Tomás O'Crohan
ISBN 978-3-03911-837-3. 232 pages. 2009.

Vol. 4   Paddy Lyons and Alison O'Malley-Younger (eds): No Country for Old Men: Fresh Perspectives on Irish Literature
ISBN 978-3-03911-841-0. 289 pages. 2009.

Vol. 109   Gerald Dawe: Northern Windows/Southern Stars: Selected Early
Essays 1983–1994
ISBN 978-1-80079-652-2. 180 pages. 2022.

Vol. 110   John Fanning: The Mandarin, the Musician and the Mage:
T. K. Whitaker, Sean O'Riada, Thomas Kinsella and the Lessons of
Ireland's Mid-Twentieth Century Revival
ISBN 978-1-80079-599-0. *Forthcoming.* 2022.

Vol. 111   Gerald Dawe: Dreaming of Home: Seven Irish Writers
ISBN 978-1-80079-655-3. 108 pages. 2022.

Printed in Great Britain
by Amazon

41078777R00063